Fix Your PC Problems for the Older Generation

Robert Penfold

D0716018

Bernard Babani (publishing) Ltd
The Grampians
Shepherds Bush Road
London W6 7NF
England

www.babanibooks.com

Please note

Although every care has been taken with the production of this book to ensure that all information is correct at the time of writing and that any projects, designs, modifications, and/or programs, etc., contained herewith, operate in a correct and safe manner and also that any components specified are normally available in Great Britain, the Publisher and Author do not accept responsibility in any way for the failure (including fault in design) of any projects, design, modification, or program to work correctly or to cause damage to any equipment that it may be connected to or used in conjunction with, or in respect of any other damage or injury that may be caused, nor do the Publishers accept responsibility in any way for the failure to obtain specified components.

Notice is also given that if any equipment that is still under warranty is modified in any way or used or connected with home-built equipment then that warranty may be void.

© 2012 BERNARD BABANI (publishing) LTD

First Published - January 2012

British Library Cataloguing in Publication Data
A catalogue record for this book is available from the British Library

ISBN: 978 0 85934 728 0

Cover Design by Gregor Arthur
Printed and bound in Great Britain for Bernard Babani (publishing) Ltd

In an ideal world you would set up a new PC to suit your requirements and then go on using it in trouble-free fashion for many years. Unfortunately, the realities of modern computing are rather different to the ideal. Most modern PCs tend to evolve over a period of time, with new software being installed, and probably new hardware and peripheral gadgets being added as well. The operating system has to change to accommodate this evolution, but each change has the potential for introducing problems. Sometimes the system seems to run into problems for no apparent reason, but the cause is probably an automatic update or an earlier change that has taken a while to produce any noticeable hitches.

If Windows should cease working properly it is not usually too difficult to get it up and running again. Most faults introduced into the system are easily reversed, provided you know how. This book details some simple procedures that enable many common Windows and general PC faults to be quickly pinpointed and rectified.

The first chapter deals with common Windows problem, plus a few general topics such as simple hardware problems. The second chapter covers problems with ports, peripherals, leads, wireless peripheral gadgets and device drivers. Laptop and notebook computers are now more popular than the desktop variety, and common problems with portable computers are covered in Chapter 3. While of most use to users of laptop and notebook PCs, much of the advice in this chapter is also applicable to desktop computers. The final chapter covers Internet and networking problems such as getting good results with wi-fi routers and broadband dongles, and getting connected to the Internet without a broadband connection.

This book has been written with the "Older Generation" in mind, who may have missed out on the computer revolution but now have to use a computer in everyday life. It is written in plain English and, wherever possible, avoids technical jargon. Little previous knowledge of computing is assumed, but in some sections it will be helpful if the reader knows the basic fundamentals of using a PC and the Windows 7 operating system. Obviously due care needs to be taken when dealing with the operating system, but the built-in Windows tools are normally safe provided a bit of common sense is exercised when using them. Much of the book also applies to computers that run under the Windows XP and Vista operating systems, but bear in mind that there are often minor differences in the way a given feature operates in XP and Vista.

Robert Penfold

Trademarks

Microsoft, Windows, Windows XP, Windows Vista and Windows 7 are either registered trademarks or trademarks of Microsoft Corporation.

All other brand and product names used in this book are recognised trademarks, or registered trademarks of their respective companies. There is no intent to use any trademarks generically and readers should investigate ownership of a trademark before using it for any purpose.

Contents

1

Windows and general problems 1

Turned on 1
Do not press 2
Safety first 2
Keeping up-to-date 4
Do not tweak 7
Careful deletion 8
Defragmenters 8
Disc bloat... 11
Severe disc bloat 13
Recycle Bin 15
Emptying the bin 16
Bin downsizing 17
Cleaning up 18
Temporary Internet files 19
Other temporary files 23
Shutdown problems 24
Non-stop software 24
Task Manager 25
Start-up problems 27
It's a Setup 28
System Restore 29
Restore points 30
Starting System Restore 32
Making a point 34
System repair disc 35
Restore from boot disc 37
Recovery tools 40
Hardware problem? 41
Startup Repair 44
Command Prompt 44
Using F8 45
Start Windows Normally 45
Repair Your Computer 46
Safe Mode 46

Safe Mode with Networking 47
Safe Mode with Command Prompt 47
Enable Boot Logging 48
Enable low-resolution video 48
Last Known Good Configuration 48
Directory Services Restore Mode 48
Debugging Mode 48
Disable automatic restart 48
Disable Driver Signature Enforcement 49
Action Center 49
Malware 52
Free protection 54
Extras 57
Awkward infections 58
Second opinion 58

2

Peripherals and ports.................... 59

Lead astray 59
Spoiled for choice 59
USB types 60
USB power 61
Fitting 62
Noisy discs 64
Paper jams 64
Freeing jams 67
Test pages 68
Failed test 70
Self test... 72
Slow printing 73
Streaky printing 75
Colour problems 76
Stripy printing 77
Spotty printing... 77
Wireless peripherals 78
Drivers 79

Making waves 80
Reconnecting 80

3

Laptops and notebooks 81

Bad old days 81
On the cheap 82
Screen resolution 83
Ideal resolution 85
Larger text 88
Deleting 90
Custom uninstaller 92
Windows uninstaller 93
Ease of Access Center 93
All talk 95
Battery 96
Memory effect 98
No charge 98
Leave it in 99
Battery storage 99
Saving power 100
Mouse 101
Click speed 103
Mouse acceleration 104
Pressure sensitive 106

4

Internet and networking 107

Getting connected 107
Dial-up 107
Wired broadband 108
Slow connection 108
Cable 109
Wireless broadband 109

USB dongle 111
Wireless woes 111
Line of sight 113
Same channel? 114
Change channel 114
Country setting 115
Repairing a connection 116
Download managers 118

Index 119

Windows and general problems

Turned on

Finding and correcting the fault when a PC fails to do anything when switched on is a difficult task. The numerous safety features built into a PC can result in a fault practically anywhere in the system blocking the computer from powering up. It is a problem that is likely to require some professional assistance, but it is a good idea to check for obvious causes before calling in a professional computer service engineer. It could save some embarrassment if the problem is something very simple and not a fault in the PC at all.

Check that the fuse is O.K. and that the power lead is fully in place at the computer end. Also check that it is actually plugged into the mains outlet socket and that the socket is switched on. If the computer has a conventional on/off switch, make sure that it is set to the "On" position. This switch, if present, may well be somewhere around the back of the computer.

Switching on a PC using a conventional on/off switch is rather like switching on many modern television sets. All it really does is to put the computer into a sort of standby condition where it is ready to start operating. With a television set you use the remote control to switch it on, but unless you have a media PC it will not have a remote control. Instead, it is switched on via a large pushbutton switch on the front panel.

This switch used to have a toggle action. In other words, you pressed it once to switch on the PC, pressed it again to switch off the PC and operated it a third time to switch the computer back on again, and so on. This method is no longer used, and the action of this switch when the PC is already operating depends on the way the PC is set up. It is possible that it will have no effect at all, but it might provide a function such as placing the PC into a semi-dormant state.

In order to switch off the computer you have to go to the Windows desktop, left-click the Start button in the bottom left-hand corner, and operate the "Shut down" button in the bottom right-hand corner of the Start menu. Windows will then shut down, and its final action will be to switch off the PC. The large pushbutton switch is therefore more of an "On" switch rather than an on/off switch, since you never use it to switch off the computer. The fact that you have to go to the Start menu in order to switch off the computer has been the cause of much merriment over the years, and the logic of it is something that is only understood by the Microsoft software engineers.

Do not press

There might be a very small button in addition to the "On" button, and this is the reset switch. This should only be operated if the PC has completely hung-up or is otherwise out of control. Operating the reset switch has much the same effect as switching off using the main on/off switch at the rear of the PC, and then switching the PC back on again so that it boots into Windows again. Any work that has not been saved to disc will be lost if the reset switch is operated. It is usually made quite small and recessed into the case so that there is no risk of operating it accidentally.

The reset button is absent from many modern PCs, which does have the advantage of avoiding the risk of the computer being accidentally reset. On the other hand, it can make life more difficult if the computer should "freeze", or not respond to instructions correctly. The "On" button sometimes provides either a reset action or a way of switching off the computer in an emergency, although this feature might not function if the computer has well and truly crashed. To use the reset or emergency switch-off function it is necessary to hold the "On" button down for several seconds rather than just giving it the usual momentary press.

Safety first

Modern versions of Windows are less prone to problems than some of the early varieties, and it is no longer the norm for a PC to crash every few hours! In fact a modern PC should go for days, weeks or even longer without everything grinding to a halt. When a problem does occur, instead of crashing the whole system, the problem is usually limited to the program that generated it.

One reason for better stability of modern versions of Windows is the improved security of Vista and Windows 7. These operating systems

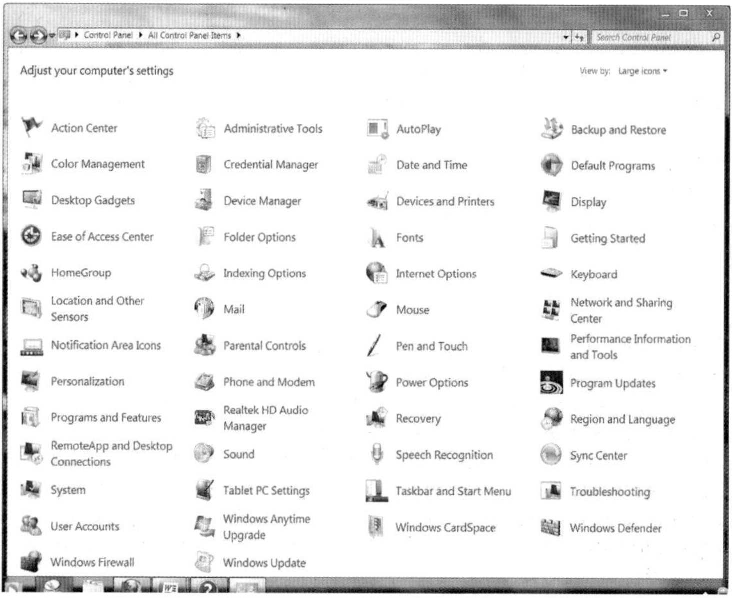

Fig.1.1 The Icon View version of the Windows Control Panel

are sometimes criticised for making it difficult for users to change some files, or even to find them at all on the hard disc drive, but these security measures reduce the risk of inexperienced users accidentally damaging the operating system. The down side is that making changes to the system can be a trifle more difficult for experienced users. Anyway, unless you really know what you are doing, it is still advisable not to change or delete anything on the computer's hard disc drive, other than your own data files of course.

A modern version of Windows such as Windows 7 also tends to be better at extricating itself from errors and problems, and in many cases it will recover without the need for any assistance from the user. With some versions of Windows there could be major problems if the power failed while the computer was running, or if someone switched off the computer instead of shutting down Windows in the correct manner. This type of thing is unlikely to faze Windows 7, but it is still better to do things in the correct manner and avoid the possibility of producing unnecessary problems. It is definitely a case of "prevention is better than cure".

Keeping up-to-date

Security from outside attack is another aspect of Windows that has been significantly improved over the years. Even so, security "holes" are found in Windows fairly regularly, and software patches to seal them are issued by Microsoft. Particularly with a computer that has an Internet connection, it is important that these patches are downloaded and installed as soon as possible. The easiest way of doing this is to use the automatic updating facility of Windows.

In order to check the current status of the Windows Automatic Updates feature, or to make changes to the settings, launch the Control Panel from the Start menu and then use the drop-down menu near the top right-hand corner of the window to select one of the icon views. In the new version of the Control Panel (Figure 1.1) there will be a Windows Update link near the bottom of the window, and activating this link changes the window to one that shows the current settings and state of this facility (Figure 1.2).

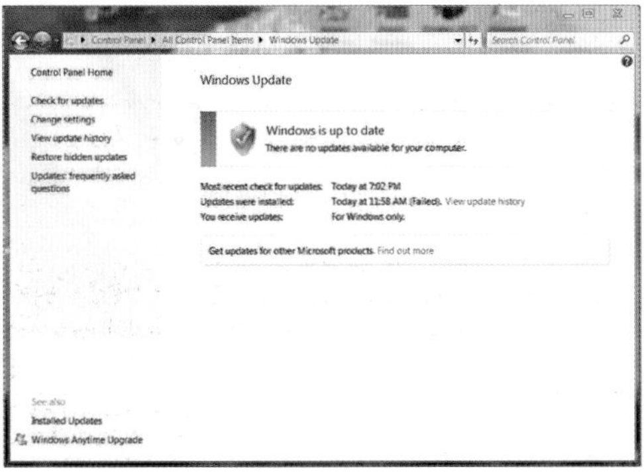

If you wish to change something, operate the Change Setting link in the left-hand section of the window. The window should then look something like Figure 1.3, but the

Fig.1.2 This window shows the current settings

exact appearance will obviously depend on the current settings used for your computer. The large drop-down menu is used to choose from fully automatic updates, semi-automatic updates, manual updates, or none at all. With semi-automatic operation you select the automatically downloaded updates that should be installed.

With manual operation nothing is downloaded automatically, and you are prompted to select the required downloads from a list. Using manual selection is probably best if an ordinary dial-up connection is used, or you have a capped broadband link with a monthly allowance that is not very generous. Pointless downloads can be avoided by only selecting downloads that are important or of real benefit to you. Note that the

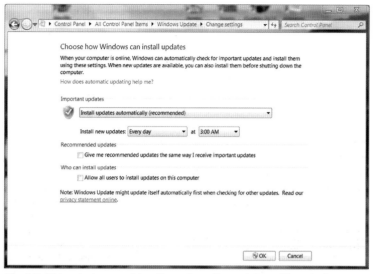

Fig.1.3 *This window enables the automatic update settings to be altered*

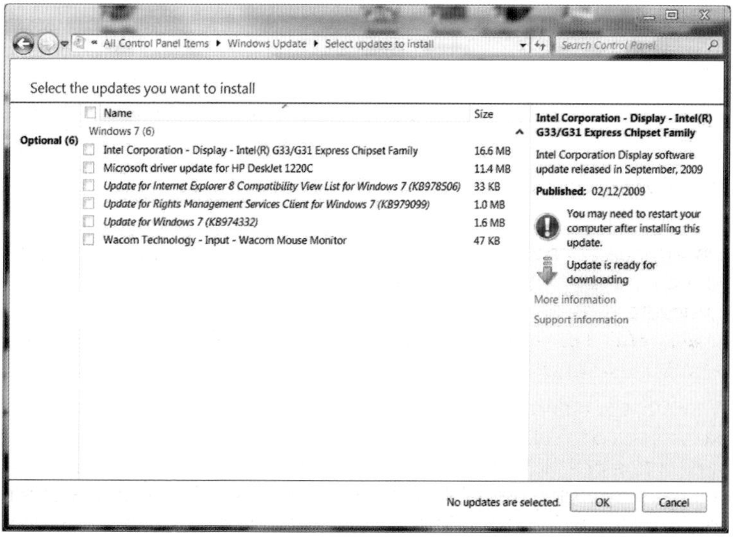

Fig.1.4 *Any currently available updates will be listed here*

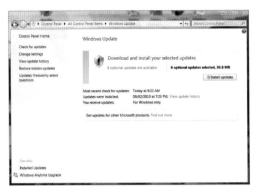

Fig.1.5 This window shows the total size of the selected updates

actual size of downloads varies enormously. Some are well under a megabyte, whereas something like a Windows service pack can be several hundred megabytes. While some of the larger downloads may be very desirable, they are probably not a practical proposition unless some form of broadband Internet connection is available. A large download such as a major service pack is usually made available on disc as well.

If you opt for automatic updates, but with only the important ones being included, it is still possible to download and install updates manually. This method can also be used if automatic updating is switched off completely. From the window of Figure 1.2, operate the "Check for updates" link. If any updates are available they will be listed, as in Figure 1.4. Tick the checkboxes for any updates that you wish to install, and then operate the OK button. The window will then change to one like Figure 1.5, showing the number of downloads selected and their total size.

Operate the Back button in the top left-hand corner of the window if you wish to make changes or left-click the Install Updates button to go ahead with the updating process. If you decide to proceed, you will be kept informed of progress (Figure 1.6). It is possible to carry on computing while the updates are installed, but it is probably best to close all application programs prior to updating the computer. Updates often require the computer to be rebooted, and several reboots might be needed if a number of downloads are being installed. Rebooting is where Windows is shut down and then restarted, but the computer is not switched off during this process. Any applications that are running have to be shut down before the computer can be rebooted.

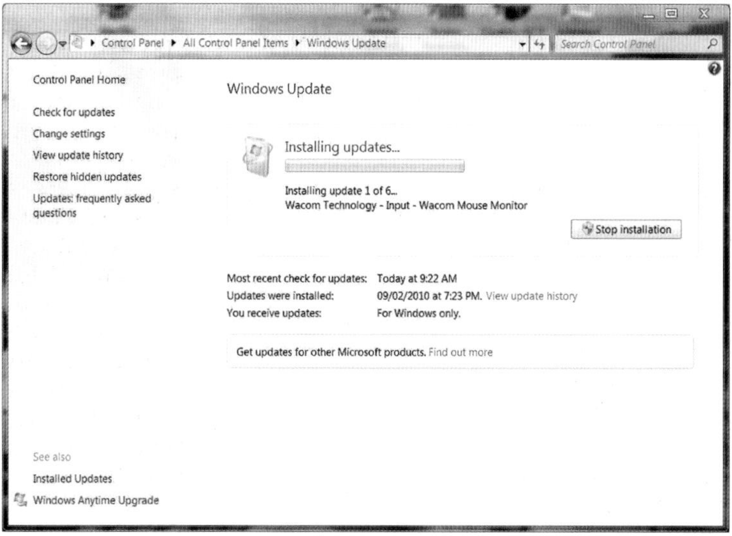

Fig.1.6 The update process is under way

Do not tweak

Probably the only sure-fire way of preventing Windows from getting into difficulties is to never install any applications programs at all, which is not exactly a practical proposition. However, you can certainly reduce the risk of problems occurring by following some simple rules. Experienced users fiddle around with the Windows configuration files and manage to customise the user interface in ways that are not normally possible. This is fine for those having suitable experience of Windows, because they know what they are doing. They can largely avoid problems and can soon backtrack to safety if something should go wrong.

Inexperienced users are almost certain to damage the operating system if they try this sort of tweaking, and will not have the expertise to quickly sort things out when problems arise. In fact their attempts to cure the problems can easily make things worse. One thing can lead to another, with the operating system soon getting beyond redemption. If you are not an expert on the inner workings of Windows it is best not to delve into its configuration files. A great deal of customisation can be done using the normal Windows facilities, and there are applications programs that enable further customisation to be undertaken without having to directly alter files.

Careful deletion

In the days of MS/DOS it was perfectly acceptable to delete a program and any files associated with it if you no longer wished to use the program. Matters are very different with any version of Windows from Windows 95 onwards, where most software is installed into the operating system. There are actually some simple programs that have just one file, and which do not require any installation, but these are few and far between these days.

Most programs are installed onto the computer using an installation program, and this program does not simply make folders on the hard disc and copy files into them from the DVD or CD-ROM. It will also make changes to'the Windows configuration files so that the program is properly integrated with the operating system. In particular, it will make changes to the Windows Registry. If you simply delete the program's folder structure to get rid of it, Windows will not be aware that the program has been removed. During the boot-up process the operating system will probably look for files associated with the deleted program, and will produce error messages when it fails to find them.

Windows has a built-in uninstaller that can be used to safely uninstall programs, and some programs are supplied with an uninstaller program. Uninstalling programs is covered in Chapter 3 and will not be discussed any further here, but always make sure that programs are uninstalled correctly.

Defragmenters

Many users tend to assume that files are automatically stored on the hard disc on the basis of one continuous section of disc per file. Unfortunately, it does not necessarily operate in this fashion. When Windows is first installed on a PC it is likely that files will be added in this fashion. The applications programs are then installed, and things will probably continue in an organised fashion with files stored on the disc as single clumps of data. Even if things have progressed well thus far, matters soon take a turn for the worse when the user starts deleting data files, uninstalling programs, adding new files or programs, deleting more data files, and so on.

Gaps are produced in the continuous block of data when files are deleted. Windows utilises the gaps when new data is added, but it will use them even if each one is not large enough to take a complete file. If necessary, it will use dozens of these small vacant areas to accommodate a large file. This can result in a large file being spread across the disc in numerous tiny packets of data, which makes reading the file a relatively slow and inefficient business. The head that reads the disc has to keep jumping from one position on the track to another, or even from one track to another. This takes time and can seriously slow down the computer when a substantial number of files get fragmented in this way.

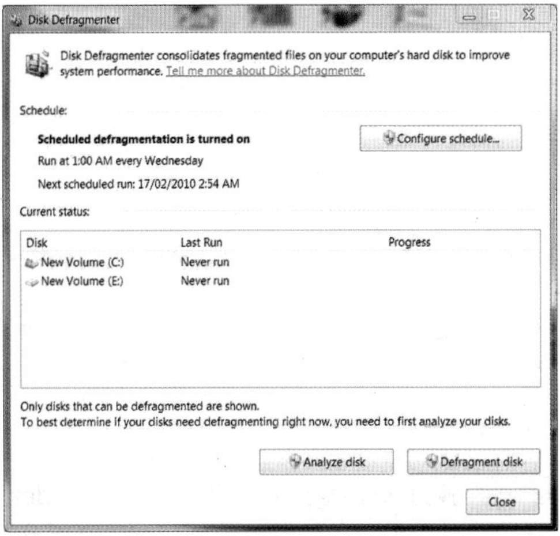

Fig.1.7 The initial defragmenter window

There are programs called defragmenters that reorganise the files on a disc drive so that, as far as reasonably possible, large files are not fragmented. A program of this type is built into Windows and is available in the System Tools submenu as the Disk Defragmenter (Start – Accessories – System Tools – Disk Defragmenter). This utility has something of a chequered past, and in older versions of Windows it gave odd results with some disc drives. At some point in the proceedings the estimated time to completion would start to rise and usually kept rising with the process never finishing! Provided you are using a reasonably modern version of Windows there should be no problem of this type and the Disk Defragmenter program should work well. There should certainly be no problem with the Windows 7 version.

On launching the defragmenter program a window like the one shown in Figure 1.7 is produced. The main panel lists the disc drives that can be processed by the program, and in this case the computer's two hard disc drives are listed. These are physically two separate hard disc drives, but it is actually the logical disc drives that the program lists. It is possible to have one hard disc with two or more partitions that effectively become separate drives having their own drive letters (C:, D:, E:, etc.).

If the computer has (say) one hard disc drive with three partitions, the three partitions will be listed separately. The partitions are treated as

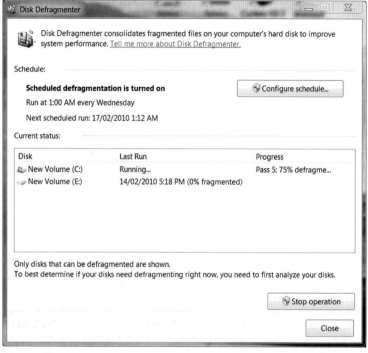

Fig.1.8 The defragmenter has started reorganising the disc

three separate entities by the operating system, and they are therefore processed in that way by defragmenter programs. In most cases there will only be one hard disc with one partition, but some PCs are supplied with a second partition, with the second partition being used for a special purpose such as videos and other multi-media files. Any partition on the main drive and other hard drives can be defragmented, but it is drive C: that is of most importance.

While it is possible to jump straight in and start processing the selected drive, this version of Disk Defragmenter offers the alternative of first analysing the drive to determine how badly (or otherwise) it is fragmented. There is little point in wasting time defragmenting a disc that is performing well. Operate the Analyze Disk button near the bottom of the window to analyse the selected disc. The test result is in the form of a percentage, and Microsoft recommends defragmenting the disc if the result is ten percent or more.

In this case drive C: did require defragmentation, but with a result of zero percent for drive D:, it was only drive C: that needed processing. Drive C: was therefore selected and the Defragment Disk button was operated. The program keeps you informed of what it is doing as shown in Figure 1.8, but unlike most previous versions it does not give an estimate of

the remaining time required to complete the task. It is not usually quick though, and can take an hour or more with a large disc that is badly fragmented. It is not always possible to fully defragment the disc, and it is not really necessary to do so. The program should defragment the disc enough to give a significant improvement in performance, and to get the drive operating at something close to its optimum level.

Regular use of Disk Defragmenter should get the disc to the point where it is fully defragmented, or nearly so, and should maintain it close to optimum performance. The defragmenter program can be set to run automatically, and the idea is to schedule it to run at a time when the computer will usually be operating, but will be receiving little or no use. In order to schedule automatic operation it is merely necessary to operate the Configure Schedule button, and then use the dialogue box (Figure 1.9) to select the required time and frequency, and the disc or discs to be processed.

Disc bloat

In theory, it should not matter too much whether the computer's hard disc drive is practically empty or almost full. The computer should work much the same either way. In practice it does not always seem to work that way, and computers often seem to operate more slowly if the hard disc gets beyond being about half full. Defragmenting the disc seems to

Fig.1.10 An external USB drive that has a capacity of 750GB

be of no help when this phenomenon occurs, so it is presumably not due to fragmented files. Possibly it is not actually a disc related problem at all, but is something that coincidentally occurs when the disc is about half full.

Anyway, modern disc drives have very high capacities, so keeping the disc below the half full state is not usually a problem. If you undertake types of computing that generate huge amounts of data, such as digital video or stills photography, it is probably worth investing in an external hard disc drive (Figure 1.10) and using this to store the data files. In fact it is a good idea to invest in two of these drives and to store your data files on both of them. One drive is used as your normal data storage device, while the other is used as backup device to store a duplicate set of data files. If anything should go wrong with the first drive, your data will still be safe and sound on the backup drive.

Having an extra drive for backup purposes can seem like an extravagance, but if the main data drive fails it will suddenly seem to be "cheap as chips". There are actually data recovery services that can retrieve data from faulty hard disc drives, but these are quite expensive compared to the cost of an extra drive. Also, there is no guarantee that a data recovery service will actually be able to recover all your data. In fact there is no guarantee that they will be able to recover any of it.

Most external hard disc drives connect to a USB port, and the necessary driver software loads automatically the first time the drive is connected. It is then assigned a drive letter by the operating system, after which it can be used just like any of the computer's other drives. There is an advantage in using a USB 3.0 drive and port as this can give faster data transfers, but a USB 2.0 drive and port should be adequate in this respect.

Severe disc bloat

While there is no obvious reason for a drive giving slower data transfers because it is more than half full, there are very good reasons for the computer slowing down very significantly if the main hard drive becomes virtually full. Modern computers have quite large amounts of memory, but they still depend to a significant degree on using the hard disc space as temporary storage space. It provides a sort of pseudo memory if the computer runs out of real memory. The genuine article and the hard disc space used as pseudo memory are respectively termed "physical" memory and "virtual" memory.

During the boot-up process Windows reserves a large chunk of disc space for use as virtual memory. Of course, it is only possible for Windows to fully allocate this space if there is sufficient unused hard disc capacity available. It is not only Windows itself that uses the disc drive for temporary storage space. Many application programs do so as well, and some require large amounts of free disc space. It is the programs that handle large data files such as video and photo editing types that are most likely to need large amounts of hard disc space. Things are likely to slow down quite noticeably if there is insufficient disc space available, or it might simply be impossible to load or edit some files.

Windows usually provides a warning message at start-up if any hard disc drive is running low on available storage space. You can simply ignore the warning message if it applies to a drive that is only used for data storage, but it should not be ignored when it is the main (boot) drive that is nearly full. It is usually drive C: that is used as the boot drive. It is best not to let things reach the stage where Windows provides a warning message, and it is very easy to check the amount of free space on any disc drive.

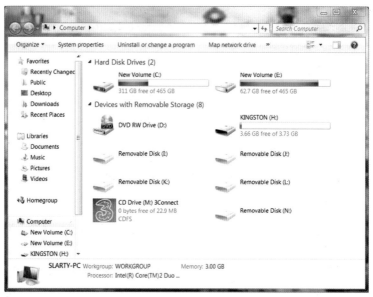

Fig.1.11   The Computer window shows all the drives installed in Windows, including things like Flash and external drives

Simply go to the Start menu and left-click the Computer entry in the right-hand column. This launches a new window like the one in Figure 1.11, but its exact appearance will depend on the drives fitted to the computer. The upper section shows the hard disc drive or drives, while the lower section is for other types of drive such as memory card readers and DVD drives. In this case it is only the upper section that is of interest, and it shows the capacity of each drive. It also shows the free space on each drive, and there is a bargraph that gives a rough indication of the amount of occupied disc space for each drive. In this case the main disc drive (the one on the left) has well over 300 gigabytes of unused capacity, which is much more than enough to provide smooth operation of the computer.

What is the minimum amount of free hard disc space needed in order to ensure that the computer does not start to slow down or become unable to perform some tasks? This is a "how long is a piece of string" type of question that has no "hard and fast" answer. At least a few gigabytes of free space is needed in order to stand a reasonable chance of the computer working well, and with a modern version of Windows I would

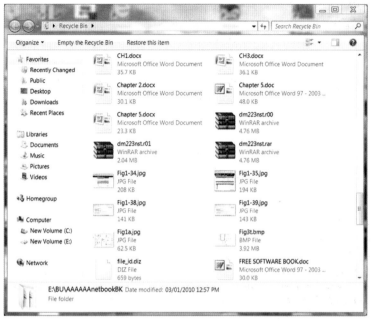

Fig.1.12 The Recycle Bin is a special folder that stores deleted items

certainly be looking to keep an absolute minimum of about 10 to 20 gigabytes of free disc space on the boot drive.

Recycle Bin

Sometimes you might find that deleting files in order to increase the amount of unused disc space is totally ineffective. The amount of empty disc space "before" is exactly the same as the amount of empty disc space "after". The reason for this is the Recycle Bin, which is a special folder on the hard disc drive where Windows stores files that have been deleted. This is a useful safety feature, since it enables deleted files to be retrieved if you should make a mistake or change your mind.

The problem with the Recycle Bin is that it often makes attempts to free disc space completely fruitless because the deleted files are simply transferred to the Recycle Bin folder instead of being deleted. In order to free disc space it is necessary to genuinely delete the files, or to delete them and then empty them from the Recycle Bin. In order to genuinely delete files rather than simply transferring them to the Recycle Bin it is just a matter of selecting them in the normal way, holding down the Shift key, and then operating the Delete key. Then press the Yes button when asked if you are sure you would like to delete the files.

Of course, you need to be careful when using this method of deletion as there is no easy way of reversing the process if you make a mistake and delete something you still need. There are actually programs that can be used to retrieve deleted files, and these rely on the fact that a deleted file is not actually erased from the disc. The hard disc has a sort of database that tells it the names of each file, and the section or sections of the disc that it occupies. This database is the file allocation table (FAT), and it is used by any program, including Windows itself, when accessing a file.

Erasing a file simply removes its entry from the file allocation table, leaving the file itself still on the disc. Using a file retrieval program it is usually possible to resurrect deleted files, but only if the relevant sections of the disc have not been reused for something else. However, it is better not to get into the position of having to use file recovery software, so either make use of the Recycle Bin, or make sure that you only erase files that are really not needed any more.

Emptying the bin

The Recycle Bin does not go on getting bigger and bigger as you delete more and more files. Eventually it will reach its maximum permitted amount of hard disc space, and it will then erase old files in order to make way for the latest deletions. However, if the amount of free hard disc space is getting low it will often be possible to free a large amount of hard disc space by manually deleting files from the Recycle Bin. Of course, if you delete files only very infrequently or not at all, there will be little or nothing to be gained by deleting the contents of the Recycle Bin.

In order to show the contents of the Recycle Bin it is just a matter of double-clicking its icon on the Windows desktop. This will launch a window like the one shown in Figure 1.12, where the main panel on the right lists all the files and folders in the Recycle Bin. These can be selected and deleted in normal Windows fashion, or you can use the "Empty the Recycle Bin" link near the top of the window if you wish to delete everything in one go. As usual, you will have to confirm that you wish to go ahead and delete the files when the small pop-up window appears.

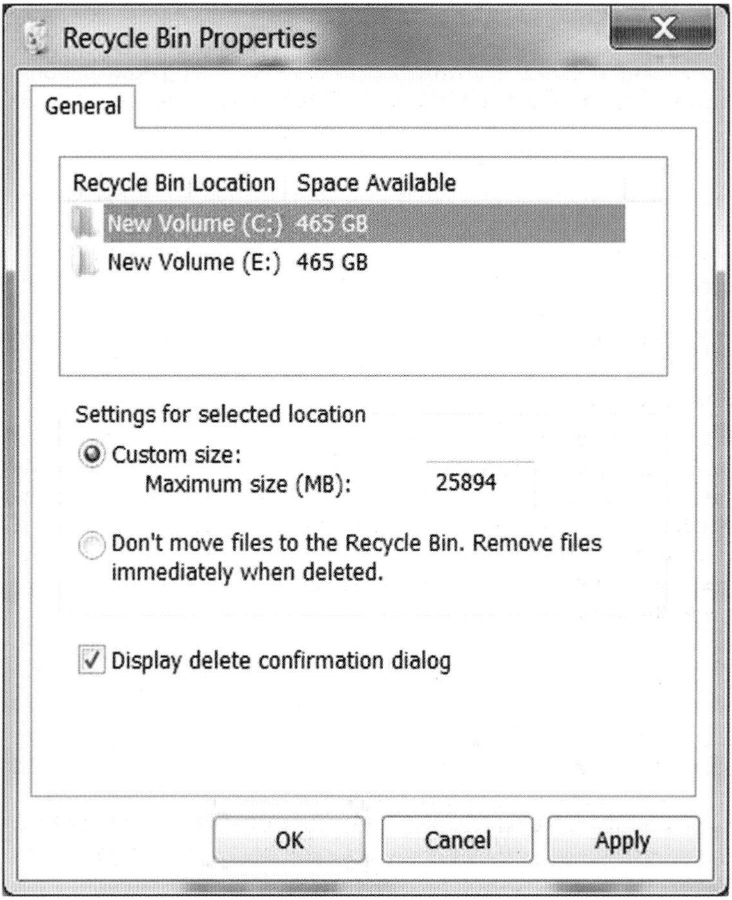

Fig.1.13 The amount of space allocated to the Recycle Bin can be changed

Bin downsizing

The default maximum size for the Recycle Bin is quite large, and this is why a substantial number of files can be amassed over a period of time, and a large amount of hard disc space can be occupied by these files. It can be altered by right-clicking on the Recycle Bin icon and selecting Properties from the pop-up menu. This produces the window of Figure

1.13, and the maximum size of the Recycle Bin can then be set by entering the appropriate figure into the textbox. If there is more than one hard disc drive listed in the upper section of the window, left-click the entry for the appropriate drive to select it, and then alter the figure in the textbox.

With Windows XP and earlier versions of Windows, the figure set here is the percentage of the drive's full capacity that will be used for storing deleted files. With Windows Vista and Windows 7 the figure in the textbox is the size of the Recycle Bin in megabytes. A gigabyte is equal to 1024 megabytes incidentally. The warning message that appears every time you delete something can be suppressed by removing the tick from the checkbox near the bottom of the Recycle Bin Properties window. However, it is probably best not to do so.

Cleaning up

Beginners at computing, and many of those with years of computing experience come to that, are often puzzled about the way that the hard disc fills with files at a rate that is out of proportion to the rate at which the user adds data files. Where do all these additional files come from, and what is their purpose. Any newly installed programs will consume hard disc space, and updates for Windows or application programs often seem to eat up the hard disc drive's capacity. In most cases though, the mystery disc files are generated by application programs or by Windows as part of their normal operation. Some of these files are genuinely useful and might even be essential, but over a period of time the hard drive tends to become clogged up with thousands of files that no longer serve any useful purpose.

Windows includes a utility program called Disk Cleanup that looks for unnecessary files on the selected disc drive. It is accessed by going to the Start menu and selecting All Programs, Accessories, System Tools, and Disk Cleanup. This might take you straight into the program, but with a multi-user PC you will be asked if you wish to clean only your own files or those of all users. If this happens you might prefer to clean only files that relate to your use of the computer, but for maximum effect it is best to clean the entire computer. By its very nature the Disk Cleanup program is unlikely to remove anything of significance, but it is understandable if you choose to limit the program to processing your own files. Note that you must use an account with administrator status in order to use the program with files other than your own, which should not be a problem if you are the main user of the computer.

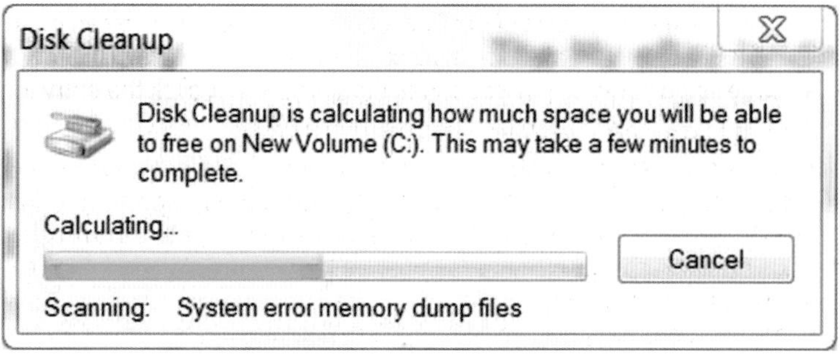

Fig.1.14 *The disc cleanup process has started*

When you run the Disk Cleanup program there will probably be another pop-up window where Windows asks your permission to proceed, and this is a standard Windows Vista and 7 security measure. At least one of these windows will pop up when you try to make practically any changes to the system, and it is impossible to proceed unless you indicate that you wish to continue. No mention of these pop-up security messages will be made elsewhere in this book, but they will probably be encountered when following many of the examples provided throughout this publication. Simply indicate that you wish to proceed whenever one of them pops up.

The window of Figure 1.14 appears when the Disk Cleanup program is finally launched, and this indicates that the program is scanning the hard disc for files that it thinks are no longer required. With a computer that has more than one hard disc drive you might have to select the disc to be processed before the scanning process is commenced. Either way, a summary of the program's findings will eventually be displayed (Figure 1.15), but with large drives containing a huge number of files it can take a few minutes for this window to appear. It is not possible to select files for deletion on an individual basis, and there will usually be far too many of them for this to be a practical proposition. Instead, you are presented with various file categories, and all the files in a category can be erased by first ticking the corresponding checkbox. The OK button is operated once all the categories for deletion have been selected.

Temporary Internet files

The Temporary Internet Files are copies of the files downloaded when viewing Internet pages. These are stored on the hard disc in order to

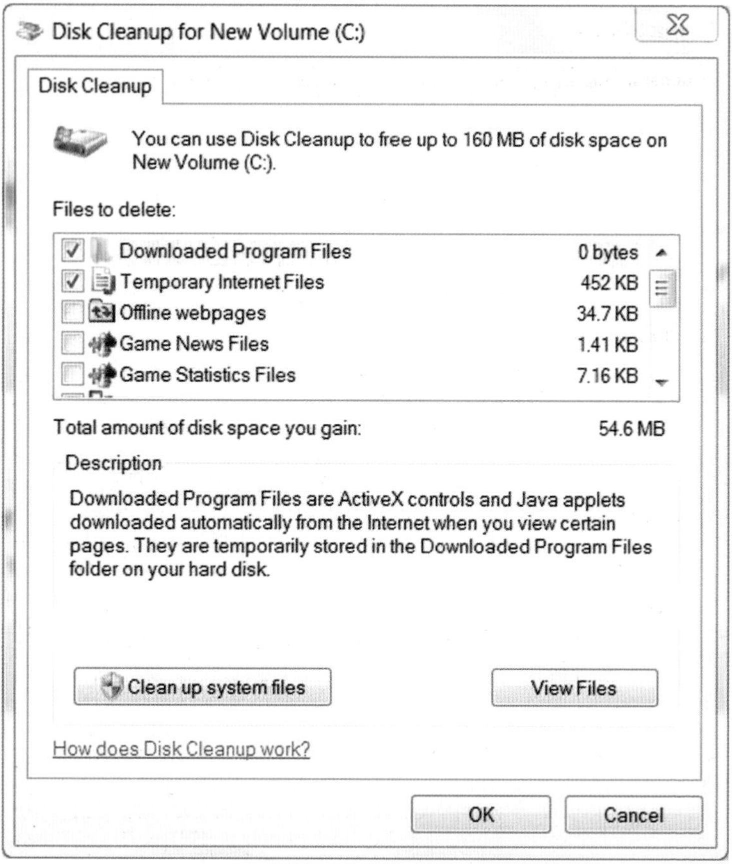

Disk Cleanup for New Volume (C:)

Disk Cleanup

You can use Disk Cleanup to free up to 160 MB of disk space on New Volume (C:).

Files to delete:

☑	Downloaded Program Files	0 bytes
☑	Temporary Internet Files	452 KB
☐	Offline webpages	34.7 KB
☐	Game News Files	1.41 KB
☐	Game Statistics Files	7.16 KB

Total amount of disk space you gain: 54.6 MB

Description

Downloaded Program Files are ActiveX controls and Java applets downloaded automatically from the Internet when you view certain pages. They are temporarily stored in the Downloaded Program Files folder on your hard disk.

[Clean up system files]   [View Files]

How does Disk Cleanup work?

[OK]   [Cancel]

Fig.1.15 The summary of the program's findings

speed up access if you go back to the same page. Rather than downloading the page again, the copy stored on the disc is used. Of course, this only works if the page has not changed since your last visit, or most of the files used in the page are the same. It is otherwise necessary for the page to be downloaded again, and a copy of the new page is stored in the cache on the hard disc. This leads to a gradual build-up of files on the hard disc, especially if you do research on the Internet and visit dozens of sites.

The files are not stored indefinitely on the disc, and Windows automatically deletes the oldest files once a certain amount of disc space has been

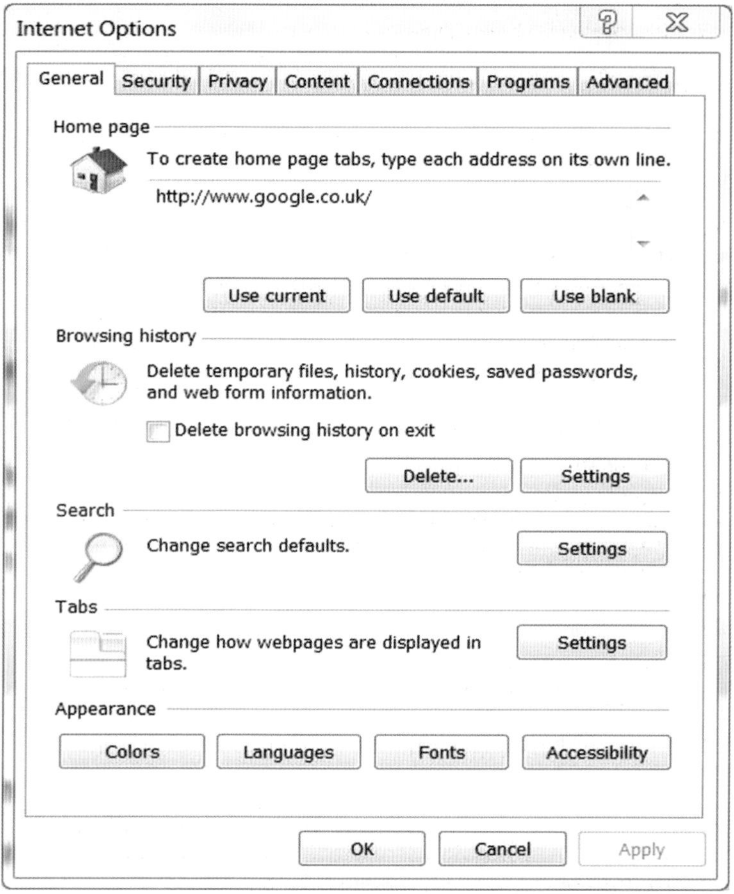

Fig.1.16 If necessary, select the Internet Options General tab

used. It is easy to alter the maximum amount of disc space that is used for this temporary storage. Start by going into Internet Explorer and then select Internet Options from the Tools menu. This produces a window like the one in Figure 1.16. The General tab will probably be selected by default, but if necessary select it manually.

The temporary Internet files can be erased by operating the Delete button near the middle of the window. To alter the maximum amount of space used for these temporary files, operate the Settings button just to the right of the Delete button, which will produce the window of Figure 1.17.

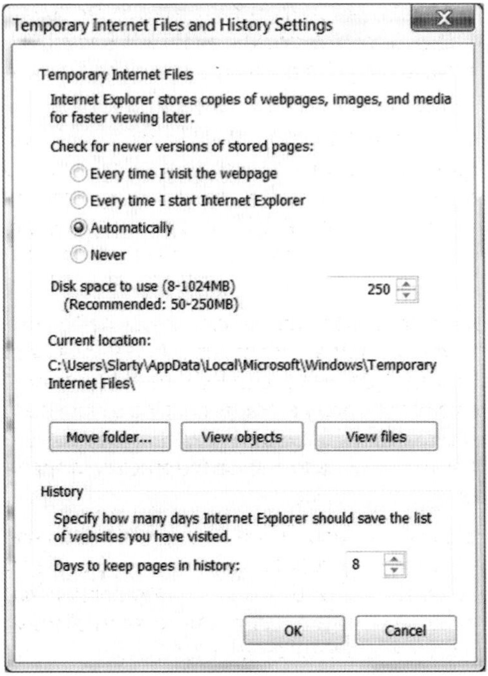

Temporary Internet Files and History Settings   X

Temporary Internet Files

Internet Explorer stores copies of webpages, images, and media for faster viewing later.

Check for newer versions of stored pages:

○ Every time I visit the webpage

○ Every time I start Internet Explorer

◉ Automatically

○ Never

Disk space to use (8-1024MB)   250
(Recommended: 50-250MB)

Current location:

C:\Users\Slarty\AppData\Local\Microsoft\Windows\Temporary Internet Files\

[Move folder...]   [View objects]   [View files]

History

Specify how many days Internet Explorer should save the list of websites you have visited.

Days to keep pages in history: 8

[OK]   [Cancel]

Fig.1.17 A new size can be entered here

Enter the required size in the middle right-hand section of the window, or use the up and down arrow buttons to set the required cache size. The figure in the textbox is the size of the cache in megabytes, and 50 megabytes should be perfectly adequate for most users. To make this change take effect and move things back to the Internet Properties window, operate the OK button in this window in order to close it. Then operate the OK button in the Internet Properties window in order to close it.

Is it worth reducing the size of the cache for temporary Internet files and deleting its contents from time to time? This really depends on the setup you are using and the way in which it is used. With a broadband Internet connection the caching system does not necessarily bring great benefits, since most pages will probably download quite fast. It will only be of real help when downloading pages that contain large files or accessing sites that are stored on slow or very busy servers. When using an ordinary dialup connection the benefits of caching are likely to be much greater. Of course, caching is ineffective with any system if you do not keep going back to the same old web pages, or you do but there are substantial changes each time you visit them.

In practice, and regardless of the theory, the caching system does seem to be ineffective when you have a cache that occupies hundreds of megabytes or more of hard disc space, and what is likely to be tens of thousands of files. If you use Windows Explorer to go into the Temporary

Internet folder it could well take the program half a minute to produce a list of all the files, and the number of files could well be in excess of 50 thousand. This gives a hint as to why the caching system can become inefficient.

If you find that your Internet connection is generally working well, but certain sites that are normally quite fast are proving to be very slow and difficult to access, removing the temporary Internet files will sometimes cure the problem. Presumably something has gone awry with the caching system, and clearing the cache removes the files that are causing the problem.

A large cache of temporary Internet files can be particularly inefficient if there is a lack of vacant hard disc space. Allocating a large amount of space for temporary Internet storage could greatly reduce the amount of disc space left for other forms of temporary storage, causing a significant reduction in the overall performance of the PC. If spare hard disc space is strictly limited it is definitely a good idea to reduce the amount of space allocated to storing temporary Internet files.

Having erased the temporary Internet cache it is likely that Internet access will be a bit slower initially when using your favourite sites. This will be especially noticeable with slow sites or when using a dialup connection. However, the cached files will be reinstated after visiting each of these sites for the first time, so any slowdown will be only temporary.

Other temporary files

Returning briefly to the categories of files listed by the Disk Cleanup program, the Temporary Files category contains files that have been placed in a "TEMP" folder by applications programs. Many applications generate temporary files that are normally erased when the program is closed. However, some of these files get left behind, possibly due to a program shutting down abnormally. Some programs are not designed quite as well as they might be and habitually leave temporary files on the hard disc drive. The files included in this category are temporary types that are more than one week old, and it should be safe to delete them. Doing so is unlikely to free much hard disc space though.

Removing the files in the Recycle Bin has the same effect as going to the Recycle Bin and emptying it. Using this option will often clear a large amount of disc space if you have not recently emptied the Recycle Bin, but it should only be used if you are sure that the Recycle Bin does not contain anything of importance. The other categories in the Disk Cleanup program tend to be those concerned with things such as diagnostics. These files are not necessarily of any use, but there will probably be little point in deleting them. The number of files and the disc space that they occupy will both be quite small, if there are actually any files at all.

Shutdown problems

At one time it was very common for computers running Windows to have problems with the system stalling during the shutting down process. In fact shutting down problems were far more common than starting up difficulties, but of less consequence. If a computer stalls during the shutting down process, the simple expedients of switching off the power or unplugging it from the mains supply will bring things to a halt, and the computer will almost certainly start up properly when it is switched on again. Do not switch off the power if the computer is providing an onscreen message to the effect that updates are being installed. Automatic updates to Windows are normally installed at the end of a computing session, prior to Windows closing and switching off the computer. Switching off the power while updates are being installed could damage the operating system and cause problems when the computer is next booted into Windows.

Non-stop software

The usual cause of shutting down problems is a piece of software that will not stop working, resulting in Windows waiting indefinitely for it to close so that it can in turn close down. Sometimes the computer will actually close down if you wait long enough, but in many cases it will just hang indefinitely. You can try using the Control-Alt-Escape keyboard combination to run Task Manager, but this will only work if Windows is still largely operational. Finding and switching off the offending program using Task Manager might be ineffective anyway.

Windows 7, Vista and XP are less prone to this problem than earlier versions of Windows because they will usually detect the rogue software and terminate it prior to shutting down the system. The operating system usually provides an onscreen message stating that a certain program or process is still running, and that it will terminate the offending software in a certain number of seconds. In most cases the software will be switched off successfully, and the operating system then shuts down normally. In a way it is irrelevant whether the computer eventually shuts down or it hangs-up. Either way there is a problem if it keeps happening.

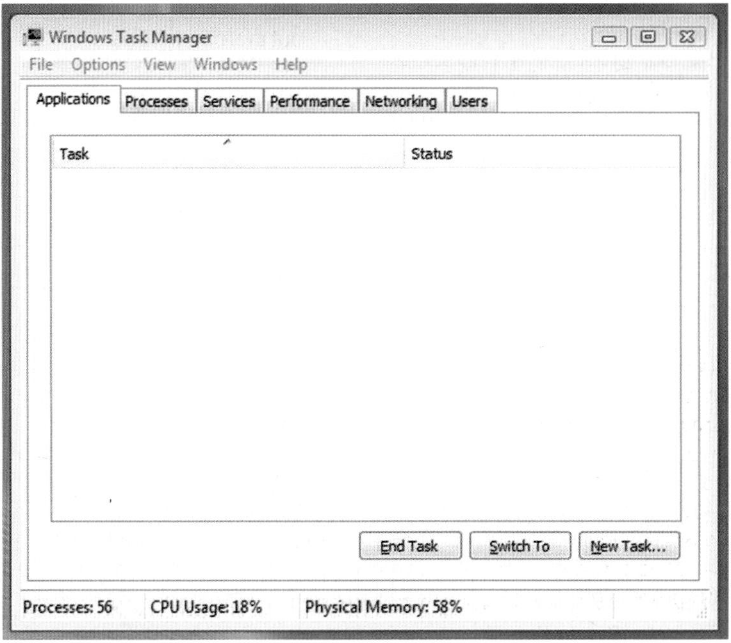

Fig.1.18 No running applications should be listed

Strictly speaking, this is not a problem with Windows itself, but is instead a problem with a program of some kind. It can be due to a faulty driver program for a piece of hardware, although in my experience this is not usually the cause. Problems with defective driver software usually surface long before you shut down the computer! It is more likely to be caused by an application program, or a piece of utility software such as an antivirus program. It can also be caused by a malicious program such as a Trojan or a virus.

Task Manager

The usual approach to identifying the offending software is to run Task Manager (Control-Shift-Escape) prior to shutting down the computer, and having first checked that all application programs have been shut down. Unfortunately, in most cases it is not as simple as looking to see if an application is still running. Operating the Applications tab of Windows Task Manager will almost certainly show that there are no programs

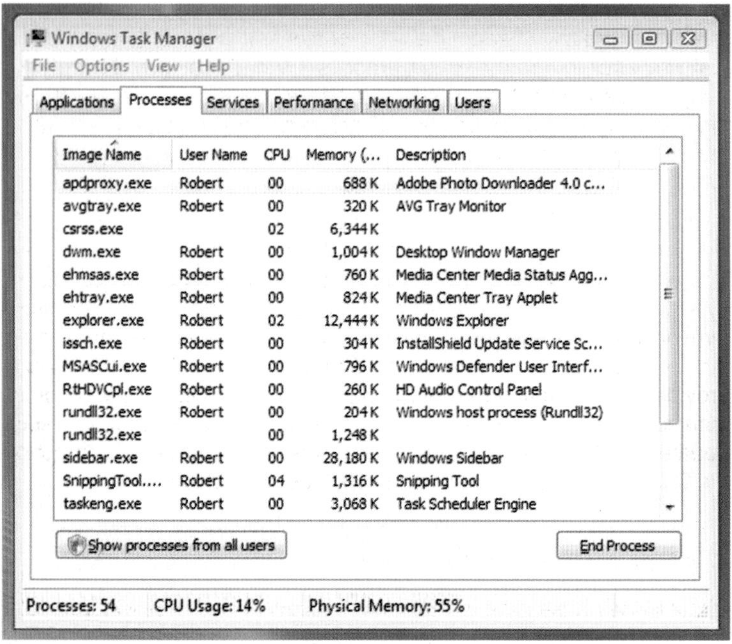

Fig.1.19 There will be a long list of background processes

running (Figure 1.18). If there is an entry here, then you are lucky and have identified the rogue program straight away. The window for the application has closed, but it is still running in the background.

It is more likely that no application has been left running, and that the problem is due to a process of some kind that is associated with an application program. The program should terminate the process before switching itself off, but for some reason it is failing to do so. Operating the Processes tab of Task Manager will produce a long list of processes that are running in the background (Figure 1.19), and many of these are associated with the operating system and will have "System" in the User field. Others are associated with application software and will have the name of the user currently logged onto the system. These processes are often something like a quick-launch utility that enables the application to start running more quickly than if it is started from scratch, or part of an antivirus program.

The obvious problem here is that many of these processes are not running in error, even though the application software that they are linked to is not operational. This makes it difficult to find a process that is still running when it should have been terminated earlier. It is often a matter of using trial and error to find the rogue process. Work your way through the likely processes, terminating one of them using Task Manager each time the computer is shut down. In order to terminate a program it is just a matter of left-clicking its entry to select it, and then operating the End Process button.

If you end a process and the computer then shuts down correctly, it is virtually certain that you have located the source of the problem. The Description field should give the name of the main program associated with that particular process, so always make a mental note of this before terminating a process and shutting down the computer. Having located the rogue program, uninstalling and then reinstalling it again will often provide a cure. If that does not work, the Support section of the program manufacturer's web site might have details of a fix, or installing the latest update might solve the problem. Otherwise it is a matter of contacting the Customer Support service to see if they can help.

Start-up problems

I think it is fair to say that modern versions of Windows are less prone to start-up problems than those of yesteryear. To some extent this is due to Windows avoiding problems in the first place, and damaging a modern Windows installation is far more difficult than it was in the days of Windows 95 and 98. Also, a modern version of Windows will take in its stride things that would have brought older versions to a complete halt. Of course, this is not to say that a modern Windows installation cannot go wrong and prevent the computer from booting properly. It can and does still happen, but it is far more rare than in the past.

It is a common mistake to blame Windows for any problem that prevents the computer from booting correctly. There are numerous possible reasons for a computer failing to boot properly, many of which are nothing whatever to do with the operating system. The first task is to determine whether the problem is caused by a hardware fault or the operating system.

The most important factor here is whether the computer gets as far as the operating system or fails at some earlier stage in the start-up process. Before booting into Windows, a computer will go through a series of simple checks to ensure that the hardware is all functioning correctly. This is known as the POST (power-on self-test), and there will usually be some on-screen messages or a splash screen during this period. It is only once this testing procedure has been completed that the computer looks for a disc drive that contains the operating system and then tries to boot into that system. There is no point in looking for a problem with the operating system if the computer stalls before it actually reaches that stage.

Even if the computer does reach the boot stage, the problem could still be a hardware fault. If the boot process does actually start but then falters, it is virtually certain that there is a problem with the Windows installation. However, if things grind to a halt with an error message stating that no suitable boot disc was found, it is likely that the problem is due to a faulty disc drive rather than a faulty Windows installation on that drive. If the problem is due to a fault in the Windows installation, the damage might be so severe that no easy fix is possible.

It's a Setup

A good initial test is to go into the Setup program that can usually be accessed by pressing a certain key once the POST has been finished but prior to the computer trying to boot into the operating system. The key used to access the setup program varies from one computer to another, but it is often the Delete key or the F2 function key. At the appropriate time in the start-up process there will usually be an on-screen message telling you which key to press in order to access this program. Once into the Setup program it is the standard CMOS section that is required. This should list all the computer's disc drives, and there is certainly a hardware problem if one of the drives is absent from the list. However, it does not necessarily mean that all is well if all the drives are listed correctly.

A drive will usually be listed as present and correct provided the Setup program can communicate with the controller circuit in the drive. The drive mechanism itself could be faulty or even totally inaccessible, but its entry will still appear properly in the list of drives detected by the Setup program. Where a drive is not listed it is quite likely that it has become totally unusable and that its contents will be lost.

There are emergency recovery services that will attempt to retrieve lost data on a faulty drive, but these are too expensive for most users, and there is never any certainty that all the data on the disc will be recoverable. It is better to avoid the need of such services by always making at least one backup copy of any important data. Of course, the lack of an entry for a drive does not necessarily mean that it is completely useless, and in many cases it is just a very simple fault such as a lead that has come adrift and is not making proper electrical contact.

Hardware faults go beyond the scope of this book, so we will assume here that the computer starts to boot into Windows, and that it then either stalls completely or seems to take an eternity to finally reach the point where the computer is running the operating system properly and is in a fully usable state. Matters are certainly much easier if the computer does eventually make it into Windows, even if it does take 15 or 20 minutes to get there! It is then possible to use the built-in facilities of Windows and third-party utilities in an attempt to find the cause of the problem.

System Restore

The problem could be due to a problem with the Registry, and using a program such as Cclean to locate and fix Registry problems might help. This is available as a free download on the Internet. However, with most Windows problems the built-in System Restore facility is probably the best place to start. I have used this to fix numerous problems with Windows, from disappearing broadband Internet connections to PCs that take 20 minutes to boot-up but then run perfectly. It should not be necessary to manually switch on this facility, because it is usually activated by default when Windows is installed.

System Restore was introduced with Windows ME, and is much the same on subsequent versions of Windows. It is designed specifically to deal with problems in the operating system. It should not be confused with the Backup and Restore programs that are used to deal with hard disc failures and to prevent data from being lost. The purpose of System Restore is to take the system back to a previous configuration that worked. If there is a difficulty with the current configuration, taking the system back to a previous state should cure the problem. It does not matter whether the difficulty is a greatly extended boot-up time or all your Desktop icons disappearing. Whatever the nature of the problem, provided it is caused by a change to the operating system, using System Restore should take the computer back to a state where it works normally.

System or program files that have been deleted or changed since the restoration date are returned to their previous state, and any files that have been added are deleted. Strictly speaking, System Restore is a program that will work around operating system problems rather than fix them. It will often provide a quick fix, but you have to be careful not to reintroduce the problem.

Fig.1.20 You do not have to settle for the recommended point

It is only fair to point out that it does have one drawback, which is that it requires a fair amount of hard disc space. It needs a minimum of 300 megabytes (0.3 gigabytes), and could use up to 15 percent of a disc's capacity. It is a price that is well worth paying though, especially with a modern PC that has a huge hard disc drive. Even if (say) a 750 gigabyte drive loses 15 percent of its usable capacity by using System Restore, even with the operating system and various programs installed, this would still leave something like 600 gigabytes free for data storage.

Restore points

The general idea is to periodically add new restore points so that if something should subsequently go wrong with the operating system, it can be taken back to a recent restore point. Incidentally, Windows adds restore points periodically, so it is not essential to routinely add your own. The main reason for adding your own restore points is that you are about to do something that will increase the likelihood of problems occurring. For "old hands" it might mean altering files in order to make

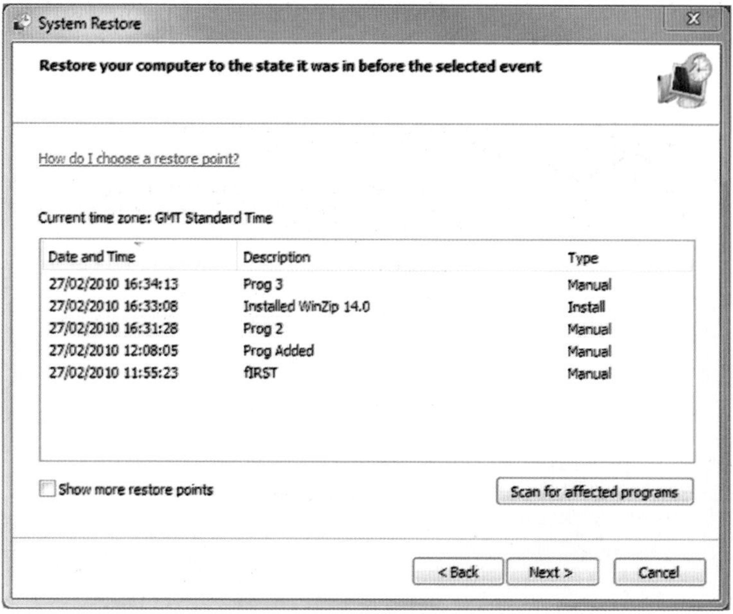

Fig.1.21 Several recent restoration points should be offered

changes to the operating system, but for beginners it is more likely to be something more mundane such as installing new software.

If anything should go horribly wrong during the installation process, going back to the restore point should remove the rogue program and fix the problem with the operating system. You can then contact the software manufacturer to find a cure to the problem, and in the meantime your PC should still be functioning properly. It is also worth adding a restore point prior to adding or removing new hardware. This provides a way back to normality if adding or removing the device drivers has dire consequences for the Windows installation.

When going back to a restore point the program should remove any recently added programs, but it should leave recently produced data files intact. Of course, with any valuable data that has not been backed up already, it would be prudent to make backup copies before using System Restore, just in case things do not go according to plan. The program itself provides a way around this sort of problem in that it does permit a restoration to be undone. In the unlikely event that a valuable data file should vanish "into thin air" it should be possible to return the

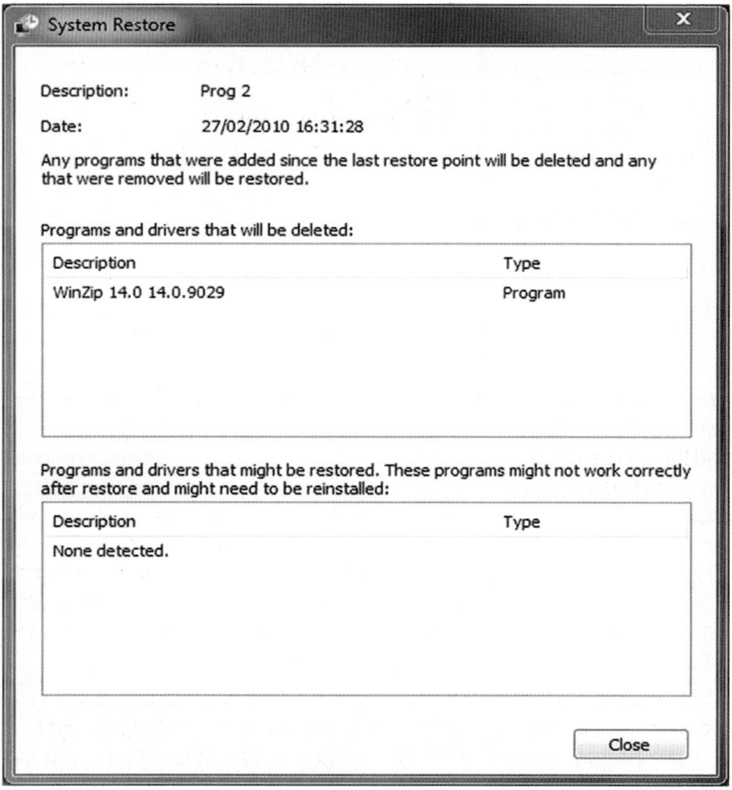

Fig.1.22 In this example, one program will be uninstalled

PC to its original configuration, back up the restored data, and then go back to the restoration point again. System Restore only backs up and restores system and program files, so it is highly unlikely that it would be responsible for data files going "absent without leave".

Starting System Restore

There is a System Restore facility available from within Windows, but this is clearly of no use unless the computer can be booted into Windows. However, there are other ways of entering this facility. For the moment, we will assume that it is possible to boot into Windows and launch the System Restore program. This is achieved by going to the Start menu and choosing All Programs, Accessories, System Tools, and System Restore. There might be a delay of a minute or two while the system is scanned, but eventually a window like the one in Figure 1.20 will be launched.

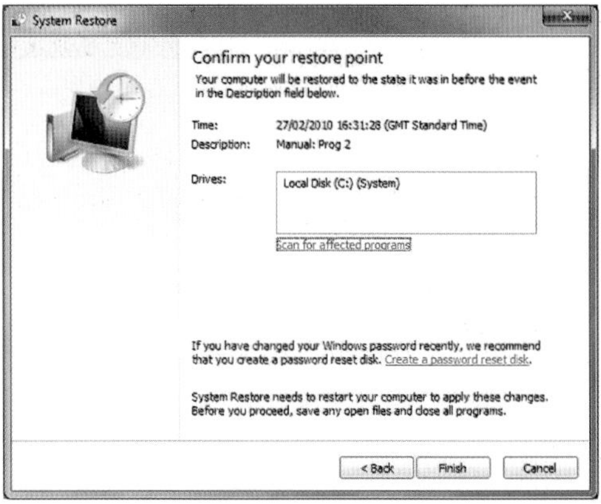

In this example a restoration point is being recommended, and this will usually be the latest one that is

Fig.1.23 Check that the settings are correct

available. You can opt to use a different one though, and this is the only course of action if the program does not suggest a restoration point. A window like the one of Figure 1.21 will be produced if you elect to choose a restoration point. Using System Restore should not result in any data files being lost, but taking Windows back to an earlier state can result in recently installed programs being uninstalled.

Of course, it could be that the problem was caused by installing a program, and its removal could be an essential part of getting the system working properly again. Even if a program has nothing to do with the problem; it is unlikely to matter too much if it becomes uninstalled. Presumably it can be quickly reinstalled once the system is functioning properly again.

Anyway, it is possible to check to see if any programs will be affected by a given restoration point. It is just a matter of left-clicking the entry for the appropriate point and operating the "Scan for affected programs" button. There will be a delay while the system is scanned, and then the results will be shown (Figure 1.22). The upper panel shows the programs that will effectively be uninstalled, and the lower panel lists any driver software that will have to be reinstalled. In this example only one program is affected. Of course, you will lose any changes made to the Windows settings since the restoration point was made.

After selecting a restoration point you are asked to confirm that the correct settings have been selected (Figure 1.23). The warning message of Figure 1.24 is then produced, and this warns that the restoration process

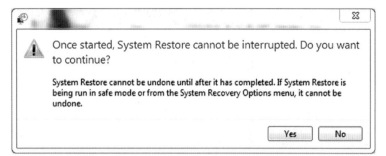

Fig.1.24 The restoration process must not be interrupted

must not be interrupted. Doing so is almost certain to leave the operating system with severe damage, and could possibly leave it in an unrepairable state. It also warns that the restoration is not reversible if this feature is being used with the computer in Safe Mode, or it is being run from an installation or rescue disc.

Opting to go ahead with the restoration process results in a great deal of hard disc activity, a number of onscreen messages, and the computer eventually rebooting into Windows. Once into Windows there should be an onscreen message explaining that the restoration was completed successfully (Figure 1.25). With luck this will have cured the problem and the computer should operate normally.

Making a point

As pointed out previously, restoration points are produced automatically by Windows from time to time, but it is helpful to ensure that there are plenty of restoration points to choose from. This increases the chances of finding one that restores normal operation. A restoration point is added

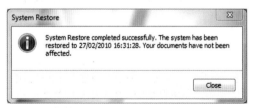

Fig.1.25 The process has been completed

by going to the System Properties window. This can be launched by going to the normal (Category) version of the Control Panel and operating the System and Security link. In the new version of the window operate the System link, and in the next version operate the "Advanced system settings" link. This launches the System Properties window, and it is the section under the System Protection tab (Figure 1.26) that is required. Operating the Create button near the bottom of the Window generates a new restoration point, and this will be confirmed by a small onscreen message (Figure 1.27).

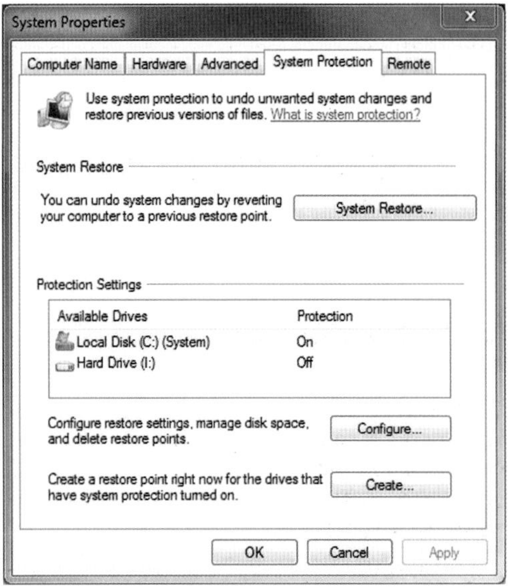

Fig.1.26 Select the System Protection tab

System repair disc

It is obviously not possible to use the normal System Restore program if the computer stalls during the boot-up process and never actually gets into Windows. However, Windows has a repair facility that can be accessed by booting into the Windows installation disc. It is still possible to use this facility if you have a preinstalled version of Windows that does not include an installation disc, but you must make a system repair disc. One of the facilities it provides is a version of the System Restore program.

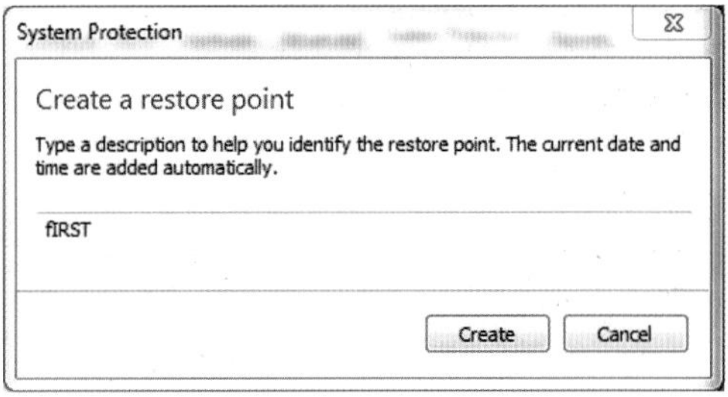

Fig.1.27 Operate the Create button to go ahead and produce the new restoration point

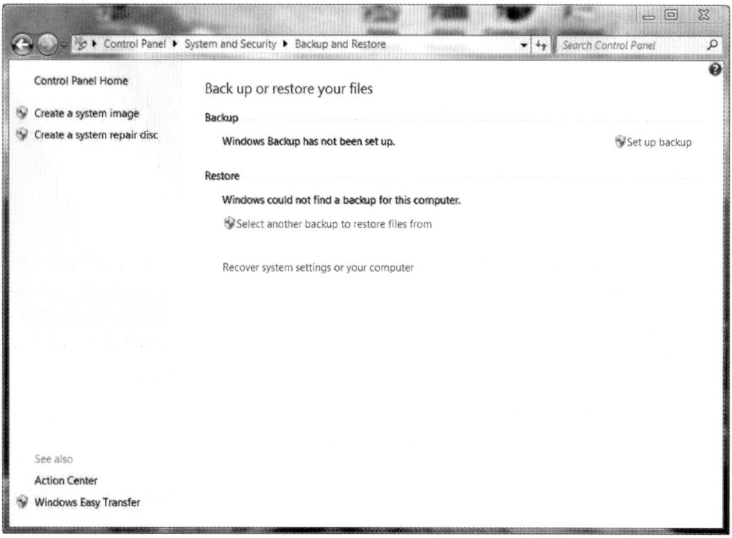

Fig.1.28 Use the "Create a system repair disc" link

For obvious reasons it is no use waiting for things to go wrong before making the repair disc. It must be made before the computer runs into difficulties, and it is advisable to do it as soon as the computer is set up and ready for use. The completed disc contains a little less than 150 megabytes of data, so either a CD writer or DVD type can be used to make the disc.

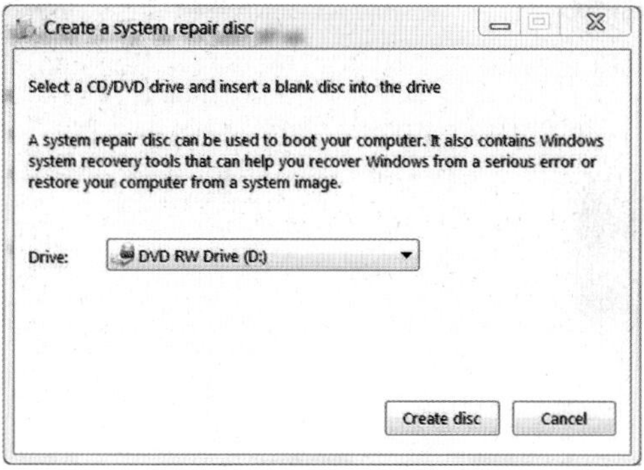

Fig.1.29 Select the correct CD/DVD drive

To make a system repair disc it is first a matter of going to the normal version of the Windows Control Panel. In the System and Security section, operate the "Back up your computer" link. This produces the window of Figure 1.28, where the "Create a system repair disc" link in the left-hand panel is activated. If there is more than one suitable drive, use the pop-up window of Figure 1.29 to select the correct one, and then operate the Create Disc button. A bargraph will then appear at the bottom of the window (Figure 1.30) to indicate how things are progressing, and with most drives it will only take a minute or two to produce the disc.

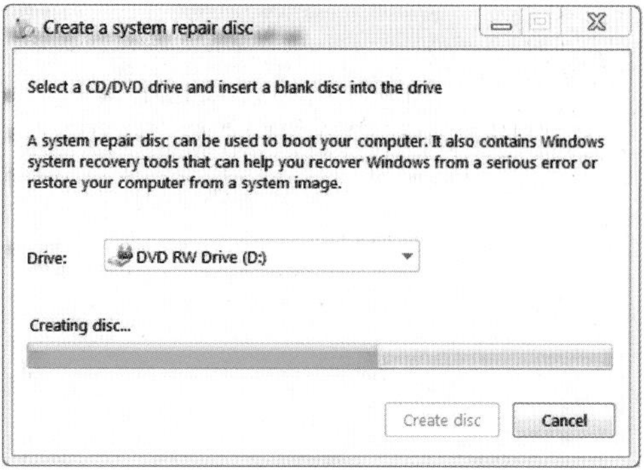

Fig.1.30 The disc is being created

Restore from boot disc

Provided the operating system is still largely intact it should still be possible to use a restoration point via the Windows installation disc or a system repair type, even if it is not possible to boot into Windows. However, it might not be possible to do so if the operating system is

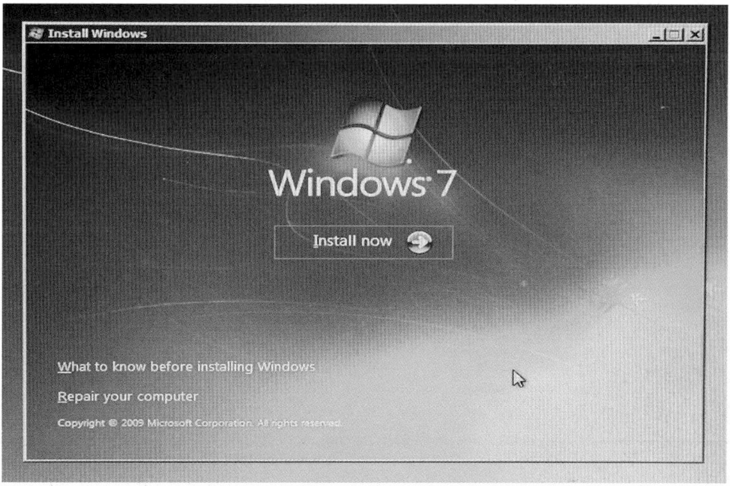

Fig.1.31 Use the "Repair your computer" link

Fig.1.32 Opt to use the recovery tools

severely damaged. It is still the first thing to try if the computer stalls during the boot-up process.

In order to boot into a Windows installation DVD or a system rescue disc it is usually just a matter of having the disc in the drive when the computer starts the boot process. Keep a careful watch for onscreen messages though, as you might be prompted to operate a certain key on the keyboard in order to boot from the CD/DVD drive. In cases where this occurs, the computer will try to boot from the hard disc drive in the normal way unless you press the appropriate key when prompted. When booting from an installation disc, activate the "Repair your computer" link when the screen of Figure 1.31 is reached. When booting from a rescue disc, opt to use the recovery tools when the window of Figure 1.32 is reached.

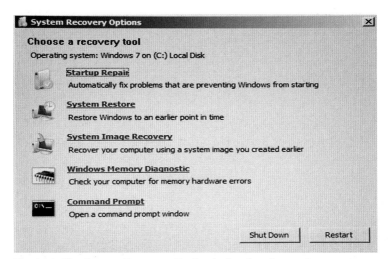

Fig.1.33 The System Recovery Tools window has five options

With either method the Recovery Tools window of Figure 1.33 should appear after a short delay while the appropriate files are loaded. From the list of options it is obviously System Restore that is selected, and this option produces the window of Figure 1.34. It is unlikely that a restoration point will

Fig.1.34 No restoration point is suggested

be suggested here, and it is really just an information screen. Moving on to the next window (Figure 1.35), here you select the required restoration point. As before, it is possible to select a restoration point and then scan for affected programs and drivers.

Having selected a restoration point, operate the Next button to move on to the next window (Figure 1.36). From here things operate much as

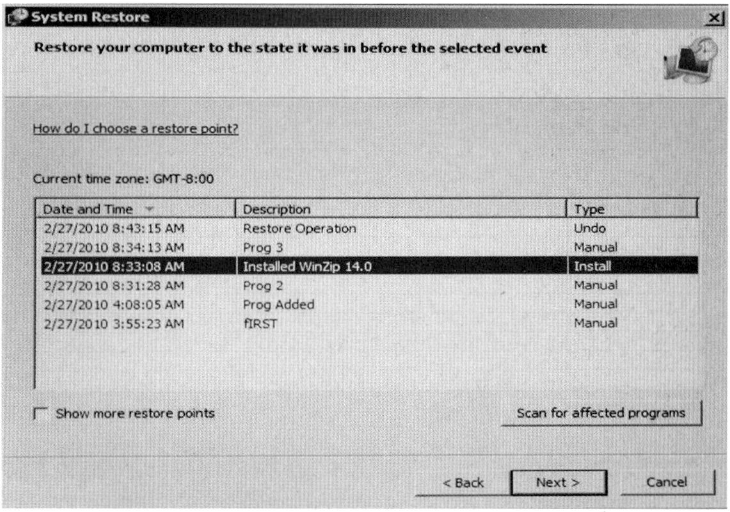

Fig.1.35 Select the required restoration point

Fig.1.36 Operate the Finish button to proceed

they did before, with the selected restoration point being shown. Operating the Finish button brings up a warning message, and operating the Yes button starts the restoration process. Note that this process cannot be reversed when System Restore is run from a rescue or installation disc. The computer will eventually reboot into Windows, and (hopefully) the computer will then operate normally.

Recovery tools

The are several other options available from the Recovery tools window, and one of these enables the computer to be put back into working order using the Windows Backup and Restore facility. This should not be confused with the System Restore facility described previously. The Backup and Restore programs provide a more sophisticated way of dealing with damage to the operating system, but they require a second hard disc drive of adequate capacity.

A detailed description of the Backup and Restore programs go beyond the scope of this book, but it is definitely a good idea to use them. The backup program is used to make a backup copy of the main hard disc drive. This is not simply a copy of all the files on the disc, but is an "image" of the hard disc. In other words, it can be used to return the hard disc to its exact state when the backup was made, with all the files in exactly the same places on the disc. The computer should then boot into Windows and operate exactly as it did when the backup was made.

Provided the computer has no hardware faults, the Backup and Restore programs should always get it "up and running" again, no matter how badly the operating system and other files are damaged. Furthermore, it will have all your programs installed together with the data files that were present when the backup was made. This is much quicker and easier than reinstalling Windows from scratch and then reinstalling your

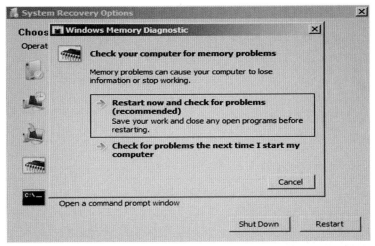

Fig.1.37 The test can be run immediately or the next time the computer is booted into Windows

application programs, copying backup copies of data files to the hard disc, and redoing any customisation of Windows and the application software.

As with other things electronic, the cost of hard disc drives has fallen over the years. Although they are not yet in the "cheap as chips" category, they no longer cost "an arm and a leg". The easy way of adding a backup drive is to obtain an external unit that simply plug into a USB port of the computer. If the computer runs into serious problems and you need to use the Restore program, the additional disc will suddenly seem to be cheap even at twice the price.

Hardware problem?

One of the Recovery Tools enables the computer's memory to be tested. This facility tests the computer's main RAM and not any other type of memory, such as video memory, or virtual memory provided by a hard disc drive. When a problem occurs with a PC running Windows there is perhaps a tendency to assume that it is the operating system that is at fault. This is probably as a result of early versions of Windows producing more than their fair share of problems. Anyway, modern versions of Windows are more reliable than the ones of ten or more years ago, and

Windows Memory Diagnostics Tool
Windows is checking for memory problems...
This might take several minutes.
Running test pass 1 of 2: 11% complete
Overall test status: 05% complete
Status:
No problems have been detected yet.
Although the test may appear inactive at times, it is still running. Please wait until testing is complete...
Windows will restart the computer automatically. Test results will be displayed again after you log on.
F1=Options
ESC=Exit

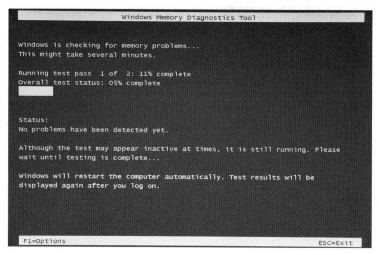

Fig.1.38 The memory test is under way

if there are occasional problems with system crashes or other errors it is not safe to assume that the cause is a flaw in the operating system.

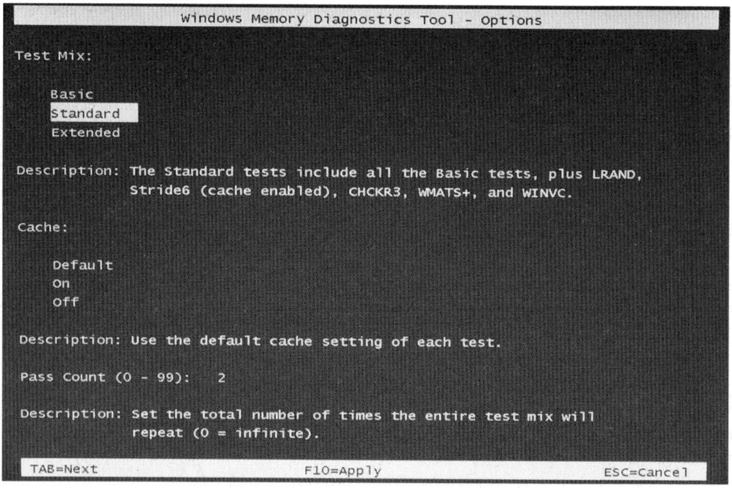

Windows Memory Diagnostics Tool - Options
Test Mix:
Basic
Standard
Extended
Description: The Standard tests include all the Basic tests, plus LRAND, Stride6 (cache enabled), CHCKR3, WMATS+, and WINVC.
Cache:
Default
On
Off
Description: Use the default cache setting of each test.
Pass Count (0 - 99): 2
Description: Set the total number of times the entire test mix will repeat (0 = infinite).
TAB=Next
F10=Apply
ESC=Cancel

Fig.1.39 The options window for the memory test facility

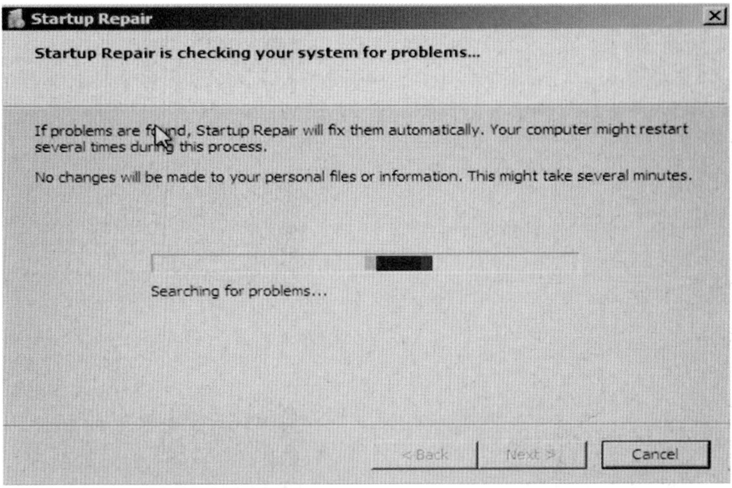

Fig.1.40 The Startup Repair facility runs as soon as it is selected

Problems can be caused by hardware glitches, particularly in cases where errors occur in a random fashion rather than when a certain action is carried out. The computer's memory is almost certainly the most common cause of random crashes and errors, but they also can be caused by problems with other parts of the hardware such as the processor or the hard disc drive. Where there is a persistent problem that cannot be definitely connected to the operating system, is it certainly a good idea to try a different tack and to make some checks on the computer's hardware.

The pop-up window of Figure 1.37 is produced when the memory test is selected, and this offers the choice of rebooting immediately and running the test, or running it the next time the computer is booted. Either way, once the computer has booted into the test program it will start to run immediately (Figure 1.38). By default it will test the memory twice, and this usually takes a few minutes. If the computer only glitches infrequently it can be worth increasing the number of times the memory is checked. This can be done by repeatedly selecting the memory test, but it is easier to increase the number of passes by operating the F1 function key to bring up the Options screen (Figure 1.39). A useful ploy is to set the number of passes to zero. The test will then go on repeating itself until you operate the Escape key to bring things to a halt.

A test report will be provided when the computer reboots if a memory error is detected. Memory errors can be caused by inappropriate parameters set in the BIOS Setup program, but it is not advisable to meddle with these settings unless you know exactly what you are doing. In

Fig.1.41 The problem was not corrected

most cases the memory is simply unreliable and needs to be replaced. Some expert help will probably be needed if there is a memory or other hardware fault.

Startup Repair

The Startup Repair facility is designed to provide a quick fix if the computer will not boot into Windows. It is completely automatic, and it starts to run as soon as this option is selected (Figure 1.40). The computer will reboot into Windows if it repairs the damaged system, but it might reboot into the repair program once or twice first. The message of Figure 1.41 appears if the problem cannot be found and repaired. Being realistic about things, the operating system is probably beyond repair if both the System Restore and the automatic repair facility fail to get the computer into a bootable state. Again, some expert help will probably be needed in order to rescue any data on the disc that has not been backed up, and then reinstall Windows.

Command Prompt

Selecting the Command Prompt option (see Figure 1.33) effectively boots the computer into the Windows 7 version of the old MS-DOS operating system. This has a text-only screen where commands have to be typed in (Figure 1.42), and it has its uses for those who have the necessary expertise. It is of limited use otherwise, but removing some of the more awkward viruses and other infections requires the computer to be booted into the command prompt screen so that changes can be made to files, or files can be deleted without interference from the malicious software.

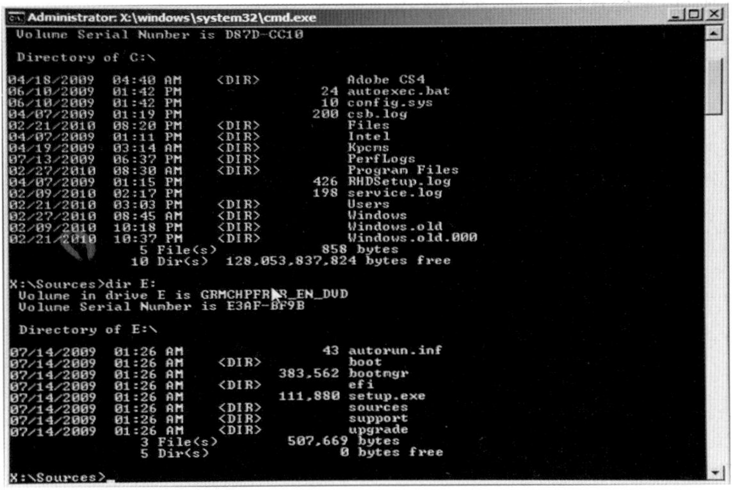

*Fig.1.42 The command prompt boots the computer into a very basic
(text only) operating system*

However, booting the computer into Safe Mode is usually an easier way
of achieving the same thing. Entering and using Safe Mode is covered
later in this chapter.

Using F8

Windows 7 provides various start-up modes that can be useful when the
computer refuses to boot properly. In order to boot into one of these
modes the F8 function key must be pressed as soon as the initial start-
up routine ends and the Windows boot process begins. There is only a
very brief gap between the initial routine finishing and the system starting
to boot, so you must press F8 as soon as the computer reaches the end
of its start-up phase. In fact with some systems the only reliable way of
entering Safe mode is to repeatedly press F8 as the end of the start-up
routine approaches. Pressing F8 when using Windows 7 brings up the
simple menu system shown in Figure 1.43. This is a summary of the
options:

Start Windows Normally

Booting using the Normal option takes the PC through a normal Windows
boot-up process, but it is obviously of no use if the computer has a major

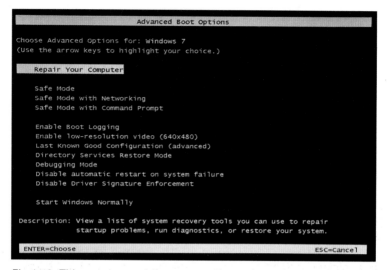

Fig.1.43 This screen provides a range of start-up options

boot problem. Selecting this option will simple result in the computer rebooting and hanging up yet again. Sometimes Windows "thinks" that it has detected an error during the boot sequence, and it might then go to the Advanced Boot Options screen. If you consider that all is actually well with the system, this option provides a means of trying to boot the computer normally.

Repair Your Computer

This option simply loads the system recovery tools, as described previously in this chapter.

Safe Mode

Safe Mode boots into Windows 7, but only a minimalist version of the operating system. The display is a basic type that has relatively low resolution, but it is good enough for fault-finding purposes. In general, the Windows 7 version of Safe Mode is better than most of the earlier versions because less of the hardware is disabled. For example, drives such as CD-ROM and Flash card readers are usually available in the 7 version of Safe Mode, but are often ignored by this mode in earlier versions of Windows.

However, there are still some items of hardware that do not work in this mode. The soundcard will not be operational, and CD/DVD writers are likely to work as nothing more than simple CD-ROM (read-only) drives. Some hardware drivers are not loaded during the boot process in order to increase the chances of booting into Safe Mode. Any drives that require special driver software are unlikely to be operational in Windows 7's Safe Mode. Peripherals connected to the USB ports do not normally function, but USB keyboards and mice will usually do so. The same is true of most Flash card readers. Startup programs are not loaded when Safe Mode is used. In other words, any programs that are normally started automatically when the computer boots into Windows will be absent when booting into Safe Mode. As a couple of examples, antivirus and other security programs will not be started automatically, and some types of Internet access will not be available unless started manually.

Many of the usual Windows fault-finding and configuration facilities are available from Safe Mode. In particular, Device Manager is available, although it will not necessarily provide all the normal facilities. Obviously in a minimalist Windows environment there are bound to be some restrictions on the services available, but those that are available work more or less normally. Boot problems are often caused by faults in the drivers for new hardware, and having access to Device Manager enables most problems of this type to be rapidly sorted out.

Safe Mode with Networking

This is essentially the same as the normal Safe Mode, but the drivers, etc., needed for Windows networking are loaded. It is possible that network access could be useful because it gives access to shared resources on other PCs, but it is mainly used where the PC is connected to the Internet via a router and some form of broadband connection. By enabling networking, and provided this does not prevent the computer from booting into Safe Mode, the computer will have access to the Internet. It is best not to use this version of Safe Mode unless you really need to do so, because any security software installed on the computer will not automatically load in any version of Safe Mode. This leaves the computer vulnerable to attacks from hackers.

Safe Mode with Command Prompt

Despite the name of this mode, it is nothing like the normal Safe Mode. It would seem to be the same as the Command Prompt mode of the system recovery tools.

Enable Boot Logging

This mode boots the computer normally, but a log file showing the name and status of each driver is placed on the hard disc. The log file is updated as each driver is loaded, and the idea is that the last entry in the file will identify the driver that is causing the system to crash. In practice, things are not quite as simple as that, but it it might give a clue to the cause of a start-up problem.

Enable low-resolution video

This is a mode that boots the computer normally, but into a low resolution video mode. This is useful if there is a problem with the video settings. You can end up with Windows booting all right but the monitor being unable to display a picture because the video signal is beyond its capabilities. The solution is to boot in this mode and then adjust the video settings to restore proper operation.

Last Known Good Configuration

This mode is similar in concept to using the System Restore facility, but more limited in its scope. It effectively takes the computer back in time to the last settings that enabled it to boot successfully. Unlike the System Restore facility, this mode does not erase or restore files. The file structure remains unchanged, but an earlier version of the Registry is used when booting the computer. Obviously, this mode will only be successful when the cause of the problem is an error or errors in the Registry. It is worth trying as an initial attempt to cure a start-up problem, but the System Restore facility is more likely to restore normal operation.

Directory Services Restore Mode

This mode is probably of no practical value to most users.

Debugging Mode

This is another mode that you will probably never need to use. The computer is booted into Windows kernel mode, and the debugging is then achieved via another computer running a suitable debugging program, with a serial link used to provide communication between the two computers.

Disable automatic restart

Using this mode prevents Windows from automatically rebooting if a system crash occurs. While this could conceivably aid fault diagnosis,

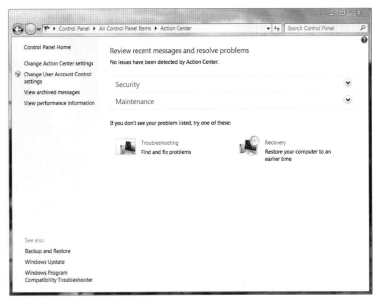

Fig.1.44 The Windows Action Center

leaving the system running in an unstable state could result in damage to system files, or probably any other files on the hard disc drive. This is not a mode that should be used unless you know exactly what you are doing.

Disable Driver Signature Enforcement

Drivers that contain an improper signature are loaded when using this mode. I presume that the point of this is to force the operating system to load a driver that it deems to be unsuitable, but the user considers to be fine, or would like to try anyway as an act of desperation!

Action Center

Windows XP has a troubleshooting wizard that can be used to help solve a wide variety of problems. Unfortunately, this was dropped when Windows XP was replaced by Windows Vista, and there is no real equivalent to this feature in Windows 7 either. However, there is a

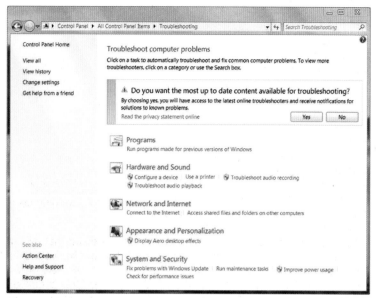

Fig.1.45 The troubleshooting section of the Action Center

troubleshooting facility available via the Action Center. This is not as wide ranging as XP's troubleshooter, but it covers a useful range of problems. The Action Center can be accessed by going to the Control Panel, selecting one of the icon views, and double-clicking the Action Center icon. Once into the Action Center (Figure 1.44), activate the Troubleshooting link, which will change the window to the one shown in Figure 1.45.

The two buttons near the top of the window are used to opt for the latest troubleshooting content or use only the standard content. It is best to opt for the latest content if the computer has an active Internet connection, but note that this option is not usable unless the computer is connected to the Internet. There are links to various types of troubleshooting help such as audio devices and other hardware, security, programs, performance issues, and Internet connection problems. Sometimes the help is in standard wizard form, while in other cases it is largely automatic. If your computer has a problem in one of the areas covered by this troubleshooting facility, it might provide the quickest and easiest way of sorting things out.

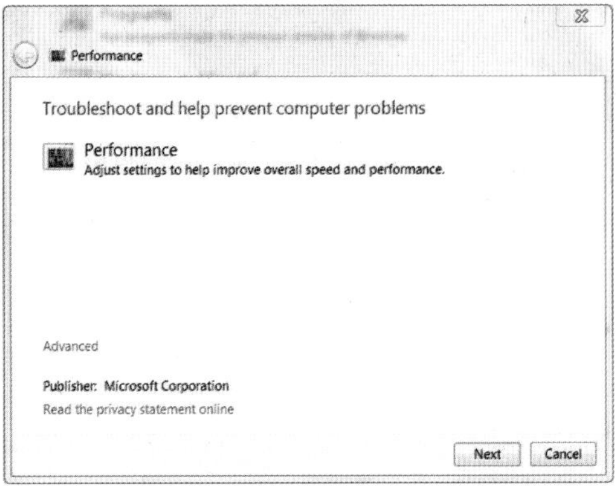

As an example of using a troubleshooter, choosing the "Check for performance issues" produces the window of Figure 1.46, which has a link to advanced options, but here we will settle for the default options. The next window (Figure 1.47) is really just an information box that briefly explains the

Fig.1.46 The troubleshooter for speeding up your PC

purpose of this troubleshooter. This is to check for problems that will not bring the computer to a complete standstill, but might reduce its performance in some way. Operating the Advanced link produces a checkbox, and problems will be automatically repaired if this checkbox is ticked. Operating the Next button starts the checking, and after a few seconds the program will either report that it has completed its task, or it will suggest a course of action by the user.

In this case it detected a large number of programs being run automatically at start-up, and it recommended disabling any of these programs that were unnecessary (Figure 1.48). Unless you know what you are doing it is best not to dabble with this type of thing, but if you are sufficiently expert to select the unnecessary programs it is worth trying this feature. Operating the Start System Configuration button launches the System Configuration window at the

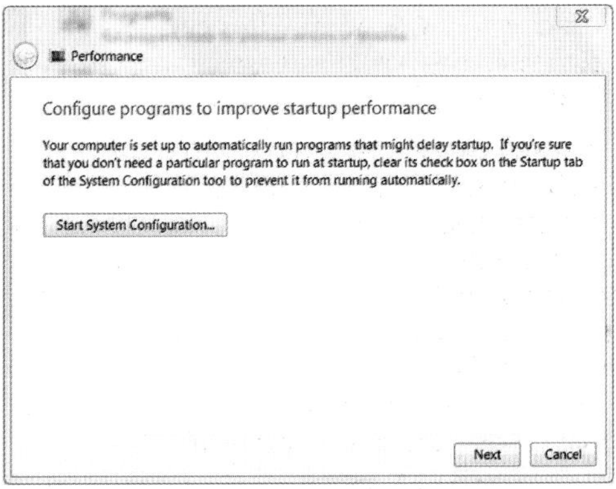

Fig.1.47 This is just an information window

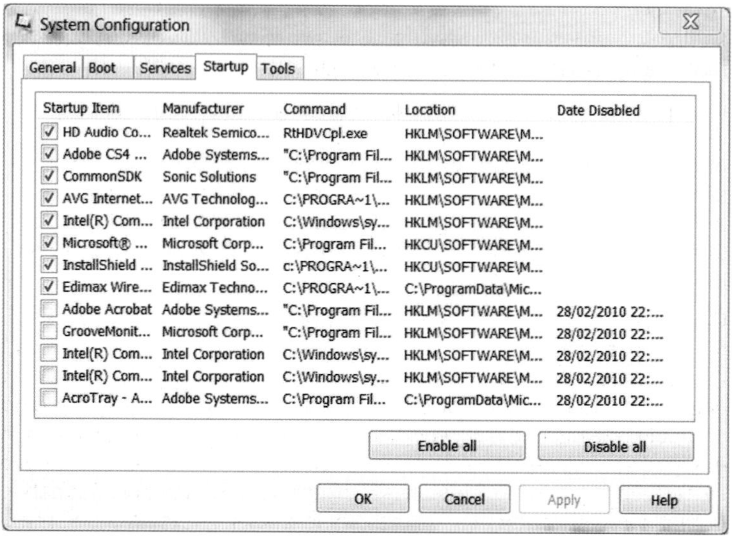

Fig.1.48 *A large number of programs are run at start-up*

appropriate section. Here it is just a matter of unticking the checkbox for any program that you do not wish to run when the operating system starts up.

Malware

All too often these days the cause of a computer running very slowly or refusing to run at all is not due to a hardware fault or the operating system becoming accidentally damaged, but is instead due to some form of malware. In other words, the computer has become infected with some form of malicious software. There are numerous types of malware currently in circulation, and they attack the computer in various ways. Some malicious programs run unseen in the background, using the computer's resources, and causing it to slow down. Other malicious programs attack the operating system, possibly damaging it to the point where the computer will no longer boot into Windows.

This is definitely something where "prevention is better than cure". Many types of malicious software can be removed successfully without causing any damage to the operating system and the files on the hard disc drive, but others will rapidly cause large amounts of damage to the system as soon as they become established. By the time you realise that there is something amiss it is too late to prevent the damage, and you can reasonably expect to spend a great deal of time sorting things out.

It is important to realise that things have moved on from what might be termed the traditional computer virus. An ordinary virus attaches itself to other files and tries to propagate itself across the system and on to other systems if the opportunity arises. At some stage the virus will make its presence obvious by placing a message on the screen and (or) starting to damage files. Not all viruses try to do any real damage, but a substantial percentage of them will do so unless they are removed first.

Computer security has become more important with the rise in use of the Internet and Email. The original viruses were designed to spread themselves across any system whenever the opportunity arose. In most cases the purpose was to damage the file system of any infected computer. Many of the recent pests are more sinister than this, and in many cases will not actually try to cause significant damage to the file system. Instead, they aid hackers to hijack your PC, extract information from it such as passwords, or something of this nature. If a computer pest is causing your PC to run slowly this could be the least of your problems! Some form of protection from malware is essential for anyone using the Internet.

Windows does actually include a program called Windows Defender which protects the computer from certain types of attack. This program is installed as part of a standard Windows installation, and it is run automatically each time the computer is started. However, it is only designed to combat a form of malware known as "spyware", and it is not intended to provide the computer with comprehensive protection against malware.

Most computers are supplied complete with some form of full security software, but this is usually in the form of a time-limited trial. In other words, it works for what is usually around one to six months. After that it either ceases to operate at all, or it does not download any more updates from the manufacturer's web site. The world of malware is constantly changing as the writers of the malware find new ways of infecting computers. Programs designed to combat malware have a database of known infections, and they can only combat new infections if the database is kept up to date with details of the latest malware.

Most trial versions of anti-malware software will actually go on working after the expiry date has been reached, but they will no longer download updates via the Internet. They will therefore work in something less than a fully effective fashion, and as time passes, the efficiency of the program will reduce as the database becomes increasingly out of date. If there is no anti-malware program installed, or there is but its database is out of date, a little warning message will pop up each time the computer is booted into Windows.

Free protection

If you do not wish to pay for a subscription to commercial antivirus software there are some good free alternatives available. One option is to use a free online virus checking facility to periodically scan your PC, but the drawback of this method is that there is no real-time protection

for your PC. An anti-malware program installed on your PC runs in the background and is constantly on the lookout for infections. This real-time protection is lacking when you settle for periodic scanning using an online malware detection program. By the time you do a virus scan it is possible that a virus

Fig.1.49 The AVG Free homepage

could have been spreading across your files for some time. By the time it is detected and removed it is likely that a significant amount of damage would already have been done, or that some of your personal information will have been stolen by hackers.

The alternative to using online virus scanning is to download and install a free antivirus program. There are a few totally free antivirus programs available on the Internet, where you do not even have to pay for any online updates to the database. The free version of AVG 9.0 from Grisoft is one that is certainly worth trying, as is the free version of Avast Antivirus 5.0. Here we will concentrate on the free version of AVG 9.0. The Grisoft site is at:

www.grisoft.com

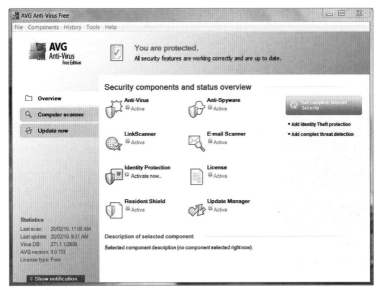

Fig.1.50 The free version of AVG offers a range of functions

On the home page there might be a link to the free version of the program, but it does not seem to feature quite as prominently in the home page as it did in the past. At the time of writing this, the web address for Grisoft's free software is (Figure 1.49):

http://free.avg.com/download-avg-anti-virus-free-edition

There is an instruction manual for the program in PDF format, and it is possible to read this online provided your PC has the Adobe Acrobat Reader program installed. However, it is definitely a good idea to download the manual and store it on the hard disc drive so that it is handy for future reference. It is advisable to at least take a quick look through the manual which, amongst other things, provides installation instructions. However, installation is fairly straightforward and follows along the normal lines for Windows software.

Daily updates to AVG are available free of charge, so although free, it should always be reasonably up-to-date provided the updates are regularly downloaded and installed. This program has a reputation for being very efficient, and it did once detect a couple of backdoor Trojan programs on my system that a certain well-known commercial program had failed to detect. It is certainly one of the best freebies on the Internet,

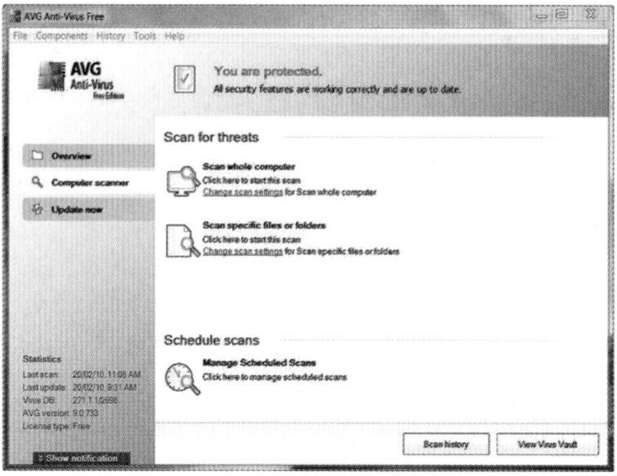

Fig.1.51   The whole computer or certain files/folders can be scanned

and it generally performs very well in comparison to commercial equivalents.

AVG has a useful range of facilities and it is a very capable program. Like Windows Defender, it runs in the background and provides real-time protection, but you can also go into the main program. It can be launched via the normal routes, and by default there will be a quick-launch button near the bottom left-hand corner of the Windows Desktop. The program has various sections, and the initial window provides access to them (Figure 1.50). There is a facility here that manually updates the program's virus database, but the program will automatically update provided an active Internet link is available when the program is booted into Windows.

In common with most antivirus programs you can set it to scan the system on a regular basis. It is also possible to manually start a scan, and you then have the option of either scanning the entire computer, or just scanning some selected files or folders (Figure 1.51). If you think that a downloaded file is a bit suspect, it is possible to scan that particular file without having to scan every other file on the computer as well.

When a scan of the computer is completed you are provided with a summary of the results (Figure 1.52). In this example the AVG program has found three infections that are actually in a single archive file. These are unhealed infections, which in the terminology of antivirus programs means that the program cannot remove the infections without damaging the file or files in which the infections are located. Bear in mind here, that computer infections are often in the form of software that is buried somewhere in larger files. In order to get rid of the infections it can be necessary to remove the files that contain them. In order to get AVG to remove the infections it is just a matter of operating the "Remove all unhealed infections" button.

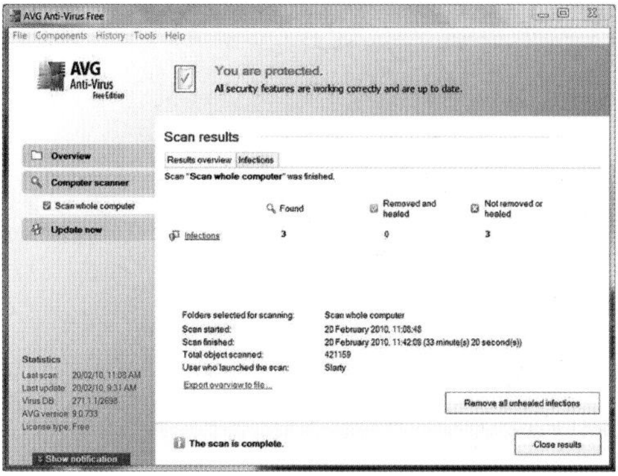

Rather than being deleted, some files are moved to what in AVG terminology is called the "virus vault". The idea of a virus vault is to render the infection harmless by keeping it on the hard disc in a fashion that prevents it from being activated. It can be reinstated if a mistake has been made and it turns out that the infection is

Fig.1.52 The summary of the scan results

actually an important file that is harmless. This is unlikely, but so-called "false positives" can occur, and the virus vault method makes it easy to restore a file if a mistake should happen. Files in the virus vault can be deleted once you are sure that they are genuine infections and that they are not needed.

Extras

The free version of AVG 9.0 lacks all the features of the full program, but it is nevertheless much more than a basic antivirus program. In fact it has a remarkable range of facilities for a free antivirus program. As already pointed out, there are various sections that can be accessed from the initial window (Figure 1.50). In addition to the antivirus feature there is an anti-spyware program, and with the AVG program installed this takes over from Windows Defender, which is switched off.

There is also an Email scanner and a link scanner. The latter tries to prevent the computer from becoming infected from an attack site when surfing the web. When using the Google search engine for example, it places a green tick against search results where a scan has shown the pages to be a safe, or a warning is given if a link leads to a suspect page. This feature works in conjunction with the Firefox and Internet Explorer web browsers and with certain search engines. It does increase the loading on the microprocessor and slows things down a little when surfing the net, but it greatly reduces the risk when visiting sites of unknown authenticity.

Awkward infections

It is only fair to point out that an antivirus program cannot automatically remove every type of computer infection. Most can be dealt with automatically, but some of the more awkward ones have to be removed manually. In such cases the program will usually provide removal instructions, or take you to a web site where detailed instructions can be found.

Some of the steps required can be a bit technical, and in some cases is necessary to manually edit the Windows Registry. Everything should be fine provided you follow the instructions "to the letter". However, if you have a friend or relative who has a fair amount of computing expertise, enlisting their help is probably a good idea, for peace of mind if nothing else.

Second opinion

As explained previously, online virus scanning sites are not really suitable as the main way of keeping malware at bay, because they do not provide real-time protection. On the other hand, they are invaluable if you suspect that your PC has an infection but your antivirus program is failing to detect anything amiss. Modern antivirus programs are very good at detecting and dealing with a wide range of computer infections, but no program of this type is perfect.

In cases where you have good reason to suspect that all is not well, but your normal antivirus software fails to bring anything to light, it is worthwhile getting a second opinion from an online virus scanner. In fact it could be worth trying a couple of them. If three different scans fail to find anything, it is likely that the problem has its cause elsewhere, and it is time to start exploring other avenues.

Note that some of the online virus scanners are basically just that, and will do no more than report any threats that are found. If an infection is detected you will probably be given the name of the infected file, the name of the infection, and any other important information. The scanner will not try to remove the problem, and it is left to you to sort things out. Other online scanners are more helpful and will, as far as possible, deal with any infections that are found. It is probably best to use the ones that will try to deal with any problems, and this is especially so if you have limited experience with computers.

Peripherals
and ports

Lead astray

In the early days of personal and home computers you tended to connect peripheral devices to your computer more in hope than expectation. Although the ports were supposedly standardised, in reality manufacturers were quite prepared to bend the rules and "do their own thing". Getting even the more "run of the mill" peripherals such as printers and modems to work with your computer was often problematic, and in a few cases it was impossible to get the peripheral gadget to work exactly as it should. Fortunately, things have improved over the years, and modern developments have eliminated many of the problems that were commonplace in the past. Of course, in the computing world nothing is guaranteed to work perfectly at the first attempt, and the occasional problem can still occur.

Spoiled for choice

When you unpack a new PC and start connecting everything together you are faced with the problem of getting the plugs on external devices such as the keyboard and mouse plugged into the appropriate ports of the main unit. In the past things tended to be organised very much on the basis of each external unit of the computer system having its own type of connector. This approach had its plus points and its drawbacks.

For beginners the range of different connectors used could be a bit bewildering, some of them were quite awkward to use, and figuring out how to get everything connected together properly could be time consuming. An advantage of having a different plug for each external component was that, in the main, you could not get things connected together incorrectly. There would sometimes be instances of two different types of port that used the same connector, but to a large extent the system was foolproof.

With modern PCs the number of different types of connector in use has diminished over the years. There are still several types of connector to contend with. Some external devices such as loudspeakers, headphones and the monitor have their own types of port and connector, but many peripherals now use USB (Universal Serial Bus) ports. In fact some audio gadgets such as headsets connect to the computer via a USB port rather than via the computer's audio sockets. Due to the widespread use of USB ports for peripheral devices it is usual for desktop PCs to have half a dozen or more of them.

Fortunately, USB ports live up to the "universal" part of their name, and they are not organised on the basis of having a USB port specifically for the keyboard, another just for the mouse, and so on. They are all essentially the same, and any normal USB device can be connected to any otherwise unused USB port. Things are easier going than the old approach of a specific port for each external device. However, it is not a good idea to do much swapping around of the way in which the USB ports are used. The mouse will still work if you unplug it from one USB port and connect it to a different one. Windows will detect that the mouse has been connected to a different port, and will install it on that port. The mouse should work perfectly on the alternative USB port, but it will still be installed on the original port. As far as Windows is concerned, it is a new mouse. If you move the mouse to a third USB port it will again be installed on that port and it should work perfectly. But also much as before, the mouse will not be uninstalled from the other ports.

This type of thing should not be sufficient to get the Windows operating system confused and cause any major difficulties, but it does mean that after a lot of port swapping you will have each device installed several times on different ports. This is a waste of the computer's resources and can make things difficult if you need to sort out problems with the computer's hardware. It can be difficult to determine which ones are the real peripheral devices and which are the phantom ones!

USB types

The original USB ports could handle quite fast data transfers by the standards of the day, but they were by no means in the super-fast category. By modern standards the original (version 1.1) ports are quite slow, and inadequate for the more demanding applications. The original specification was therefore updated to version 2.0, which was much faster. Now version 2.0 has been superseded by the USB 3.0 standard. Any reasonably modern PC should have at least version 2.0, but will not necessarily have USB 3.0 ports.

The more basic USB devices such as keyboards and mice will work quite happily with any USB port, so you do not need to worry too much which particular type your computer is equipped with. Some of the more complex devices such as digital cameras and scanners will only work with USB 2.0 or USB 3.0 ports, while others will also work with USB 1.1 ports, but only at reduced speed. Unless you are using a really old second-hand PC it should have at least USB 2.0 ports, and there should be no problems with incompatibility or slow operation when using USB 2.0 devices. USB 3.0 is only required for some specialist applications such as digital video. However, if a device requires a USB 3.0 port it is unlikely that it will work with a USB 2.0 or 1.1 type, even in a limited fashion. Before buying any USB 3.0 gadget it is essential to check the specification of your computer to ensure that it does actually have at least one USB port of this type.

USB power

Some USB devices are powered from the host computer via the USB port, while others have their own power source. Where a USB gadget has its own power source it is mostly in the form of an external mains power supply, but it can also be an internal mains power supply or batteries. In some cases there is the option of using an external supply unit or powering the unit from the USB port. Another variation is where a USB add-on has a sort of double USB cable and plugs for two ports. This is where the power from a single port is inadequate to power the unit, so it uses power from a second port in order to make up the shortfall. With devices of this type there is usually the option of using a mains power supply unit instead of power from the computer.

In an ideal world every USB port would be able to supply the full quota of power, and plugging any USB powered device into any PC would guarantee that there would be no problems with inadequate power. In the real world problems can occur with a device failing to work, possibly with a little pop-up message appearing on the computer's screen to explain that the peripheral device you are trying to use requires more power than the port can provide.

This type of thing is most likely to occur when using a portable PC. It is not realistic to expect the battery of a netbook or laptop computer to power the computer itself plus several power-hungry gadgets via the USB ports. The battery would run flat in a few minutes. Some portable PCs have one USB port that can provide power to the more complex

USB gadgets, and (say) three more that can be used with low power peripherals or those that have their own power source.

Power supply problems are also likely to occur when using a simple USB hub. This is a gadget that connects to one of the computer's USB ports, and effectively splits to provide several USB ports. Unfortunately, with the more simple hubs the power available from the single USB port of the computer is shared amongst the USB ports provided by the hub. Although a USB peripheral gadget may work perfectly well when it is plugged directly into one of the computer's USB ports, it will not necessarily do so if it is used via a simple hub. There will obviously be no problem with USB devices that have their own power source, and low-power devices such as mice and card readers are unlikely to give any difficulties either.

USB power problems can sometimes be avoided by making sure that any peripheral gadgets that draw little or no power from the USB ports are used with ports that are only intended for low power devices, leaving the USB ports that can provide higher output powers available for the gadgets that need them. Of course, this approach is not applicable if the number of high-power gadgets is greater than the number of available USB ports that are fully specified. In such cases the solution is to use a powered USB hub. Unlike the very simple hubs, a powered type has its own power supply unit and all its USB ports should be capable of powering any USB gadget. A powered hub is not reliant on power from the computer at all, and a device of this type can be used with any USB port.

Fitting

"It does not fit" is a common complaint when newcomers to the world of computing try to connect everything together. The computer manufacturers' help lines apparently receive numerous calls from the owners of new PCs who cannot get one item or another connected to the base unit. An important point to bear in mind is that the orientation of plugs is often important. There are exceptions, such as the miniature jack plugs that are often used in computer audio systems, but in most cases a plug will not fit if it is upside-down, or even if it is rotated a few degrees from the correct orientation.

The correct orientation often becomes obvious if you look carefully at both connectors. This is not always the case though, and it is often difficult to get a really good look at the connectors tucked away at the back of a PC. If you look at a USB plug you will see that it has one half solid and the other half hollow (Figure 2.1). The connector on the PC

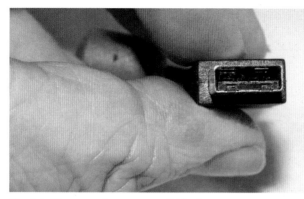

*Fig.2.1   The complementary solid/hollow construction of a USB
connector ensures that it can only be fitted the right way up*

has a complementary arrangement that makes it impossible to fit the plug upside-down.

If it is not possible to see the connector on the PC properly, just try the plug one way, and if that fails, try the opposite orientation. The "hammer and tongs" approach is not the right one with electronic equipment, and attempting to force plugs into sockets is likely to damage something. A plug will fit into a socket once the orientation is correct. It will not fit into a socket properly if the orientation is not correct, and shoving a bit harder will not change that fact. It might damage one of the connectors though, and this type of thing is unlikely to be covered by the guarantee. New connectors are notorious for being a bit reluctant to fit together, but some wiggling and no more than firm pressure is more likely to be successful than using brute force.

It used to be quite common for computer connectors to have two screws that locked them into place, but this way of doing things seems to have largely fallen from favour. The connectors used for video outputs still use this system though. It is a feature of the old VGA 15-pin connector (Figure 2.2 - left) and the newer DVI type (Figure 2.2 - right). A proper connection will still be made if the plug on the monitor's lead is fully pushed into position on the computer's video output, but due to the weight and stiffness of most monitor cables, the connector will tend to keep falling out of place. It is presumably for this reason that the fixing screws are still used for video connectors.

If there is a lack of any response from the monitor when using a computer for the first time it is definitely a good idea to check that the monitor's

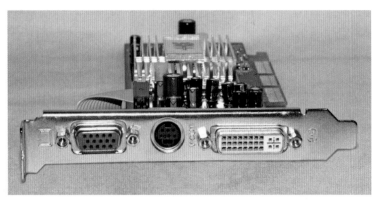

Fig.2.2 A VGA port (left) and a DVI type (right)

cable is fitted to the PC correctly. It can sometimes seem as though the plug is connected properly to the port on the computer because the two screws are tightly in place, but the plug is actually skewed slightly and is not making contact at both ends. Make sure that the plug is fully pushed home before tightening the fixing screws. The two screws usually have slots to take the blade of a screwdriver, but they are also fitted with plastic finger grips so that they can be adequately tightened by hand.

Noisy discs

If you place a disc into a CD-ROM or DVD drive, and it sounds rather like a thunderstorm as soon as the disc starts to rotate, do not assume that the drive has had a catastrophic failure. The most likely cause of the problem is that you have put a second disc in the drive without removing the first disc! Another possible cause is that you have used the last CD-R from a bulk pack of the type that has the disc on a long spindle. There is usually a clear plastic disc at the bottom of the pack, and this often sticks to the disc at the bottom of the pile. Pandemonium results if you fail to notice this and put the two discs in the drive. Fortunately, although it sounds as though the drive and the discs are self-destructing, in most cases they all seem to come through the experience largely unscathed.

Paper jams

Of the common computer peripherals, I think it is fair to say that printers are probably the most troublesome. In the early days of home computing the main problem was actually getting the printer connected to the computer in a suitable fashion. Better standardisation of modern computer ports has removed this problem. Things should go well initially provided you make sure that the driver software you are using is the latest version for the operating system in use, and the manufacturer's installation instructions are followed correctly. However, matters are not always straightforward once you start printing.

To the cynics of this world, computer printers are the perfect example of modern technology in action. They use hi-tech electronics and mechanical engineering to produce perfectly formed text characters and superb colour prints that can rival high quality photographic prints. At least they do if you can actually get the paper to load and run through the printer correctly!

The paper getting jammed in printers was a common problem in the early days of personal computing, and it is an aspect of computing that seems to have made little progress over the years. Most of the problems with early printers centred on fanfold paper used with tractor feeds. This type of paper feed is little used these days, and it is automatic sheet feeders that are responsible for most of the difficulties with modern printers. The usual problem is that several sheets of paper stick together. There is no major problem when a couple of sheets occasionally stick together. You simply get the odd blank page mixed in with the printed pages. Things are more serious if several sheets stick together, since this can "gum up the works" and produce a serious paper jam. This problem can usually be avoided by running your thumb down each edge of the block of paper before loading it into the printer. Thumbing through the paper should separate any sheets that have stuck together at the edges.

The wrong paper setting is another common cause of paper jams. Setting the printer for use with thin paper and then using thick paper, film, or envelopes is the less dire mistake. It could result in a paper jam, but in most cases the feed mechanism will simply fail to load anything. Results are likely to be less happy if the printer is left at a setting for thick media and then used with thin paper. I had an printer that our cats found irresistible as a bed, and they would frequently knock the paper thickness lever from its thinnest setting to the thickest. If no one noticed that the setting had changed, a paper jam would soon follow. About 20 or 30 sheets of paper would start to feed into the printer, but the feed mechanism would jam with the paper about 25 percent of the way into the printer.

Unfortunately, the printer would do its best to continue feeding the paper through, printing away on the same strip of paper which soon became

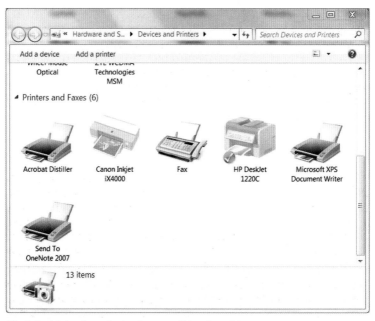

Fig.2.3 All the installed printers will be listed here

drenched with ink. This is typical of paper jams caused by an incorrect paper setting. In trying to force a block of paper through the printer, the feed mechanism can self-destruct. In the case of my inkjet printer, parts of the mechanism became distorted, and eventually it could only be used with single sheets of paper. It is therefore important to avoid paper jams in general, and this type of jam in particular.

Probably the most common cause of paper jams is using paper that is thicker than the printer is designed to handle. Paper is normally graded on the basis of its weight in grams per square metre, which is normally abbreviated to just "gsm". It might seem reasonable to risk (say) 360gsm paper if the printer is rated as usable with up to 320gsm paper, but practical experience suggests that doing so is likely to give problems. In fact an exceptionally stiff 320gsm paper might only go through the printer with some minor difficulties, or it might even fail to feed through properly and jam. Ideally you should use paper that is comfortably within the maximum rating of the printer.

Another point to bear in mind is that thicker papers and envelopes might not be usable with the normal sheet feeder. They sometimes have to be used with a different paper path so that they take a straighter route through the printer. Even if thicker media can be used with the normal paper path, it might be necessary to use one sheet at a time rather than the usual stack of sheets. Check the instruction manual to find the correct procedure before using any heavy grade of paper, envelopes, transparent media, or anything that is out of the ordinary.

Freeing jams

When a paper jam occurs it is essential to switch off the printer as quickly as possible and disconnect it from the mains supply. This prevents the paper feed mechanism from doing any more damage, and makes it safe to start removing the jammed paper. Switching off the printer will get Windows confused, with the printer suddenly failing to respond. An error message might appear on the screen. It is advisable to use the Cancel option and terminate the print job, if the message includes this option.

Alternatively, go to the Start menu and select the Devices and Printers option, which will be in the right-hand section of the menu and not in the list of programs. Scroll down to the bottom of the new window that appears, and here there will be a list of the installed printers. In the example of Figure 2.3 there are several printers listed, and you may well find that there is more than the single printer that is connected to your computer. Any additional printers will either be default types included as part of the Windows installation, or they will be "virtual" printers associated with application programs that you have installed. Just ignore the entries for any printers other than the one you are trying to use.

You can obtain a list of current print jobs by first double-clicking the icon for the printer you are using, and then double-clicking the "See what's printing" section in the new window that appears (Figure 2.4). This will produce a small window that includes an entry for the stalled print job. Right-click the entry and then select Cancel from the pop-up menu (Figure 2.5). With some of the pages damaged, there is no realistic prospect of finishing the current printing job. Instead, it is a matter of salvaging as many of the completed pages as possible, and then printing the other pages. The Print window permits a specified range of pages to be printed, so there is no need to print all the pages again if the initial pages from the first print run are all right.

It is prudent to consult the printer's instruction manual before trying to remove the paper that is stuck in the printer. This should offer some

Fig.2.4 Double-click the "See what's printing" link

guidance about the easiest way of removing the paper, and it might include some warnings about things that you must not do in order to avoid damaging the printer. In general, the best way to remove the paper is to pull it back out of the printer, rather than trying to get it to go through the printer following the normal paper path. Trying to move the paper forwards is likely to jam it more tightly, making matters much worse. Get the best grip you can on the paper and then pull it firmly and steadily. Usually, this will slowly but steadily unwind the paper until it pulls free. Jerking the paper will probably result in it tearing, leaving you relatively little to get hold of. The slow but steady approach is more likely to have the desired effect.

Test pages

It can be useful to print test pages in situations where the printer is connected up and rearing to go, the printer's drivers are installed, but the printer will not actually print anything. A test page can usually be

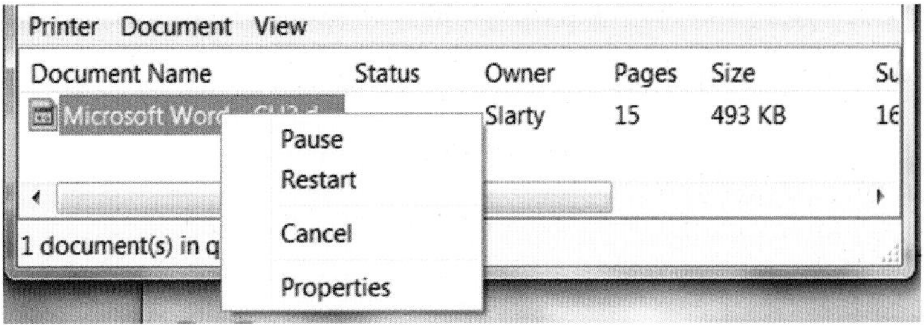

Printer Document View						
Document Name	Status	Owner	Pages	Size		Su
Microsoft Word		Slarty	15	493 KB		16

Pause
Restart
Cancel
Properties

1 document(s) in q

Fig.2.5 Select the Cancel option from the menu

printed during the Windows installation process, and it is a good idea to choose this option as it will make any problems clear from the outset.

The page produced varies from one printer to another, but typically there is a small graphic and a message at the top of the page. Further down the page there might be something like a colour test section and some technical information about the printer's drivers and installation. It is usually pretty obvious if things have gone wrong. In most cases nothing at all will be printed, or the printer will produce garbage.

The first step when printing a test page is to go to the Devices and Printers window as before (Figure 2.3), and then right-click the icon for the appropriate printer. Next choose Properties or Printer Properties from the pop-up menu. This brings up the Properties window for the printer, and this window varies from one printer to another, but under the General tab there might be a button marked "Print Test Page". Operating this button should result in the test page being printed, but note that this option is not present for all printers. Printers are often supplied complete with a utility program that enables a test sheet to be printed.

There is nothing wrong with the printer drivers, the printer, or the connecting cable, if the page is printed correctly. Try printing from a Windows application again, but this time make sure that the correct printer is selected. You can change the default printer by going to the Devices and Printers window, right-clicking on the printer you wish to set as the default unit, and then selecting "Set as Default Printer" from the pop-up menu. There is a tick shown against the default printer's icon in the Printers window, and in Figure 2.3 it is the HP DeskJet 1220C that is set as the default printer. The standard Windows printing facilities enable the required printer to be selected when printing documents, so make sure that the correct printer is selected when printing from application programs. This setting will override the default setting in the Printers window.

Check the other settings if the correct printer is selected and the printer is still not functioning correctly. Is the page range valid, or are you trying to print pages that do not exist? Does the paper size match the paper that you are actually using? Modern printers tend to have numerous options available, and these can be accessed via the Properties button when in an application program's Print window. The settings available here clearly have to match the facilities of the printer, and they are therefore different for each model. However, there is usually a section that controls the resolution, and there may be other settings that govern the paper type, use of toner or ink saving, and others aspects of the print quality. Is the printer producing poor quality results because it is set to a low-resolution mode so as to use as little ink or toner as possible?

When the test page is printed properly but an application does not produce any output from the printer, there is a strong possibility that it is the application rather than Windows or the printer that is at fault. The easy way to check this point is to open another application, produce a quick test document, and then try to print it. Any print jobs currently in the print queue should be cancelled first, so that they cannot block the new print job. If the printer works properly with all but one application, clearly that application is faulty.

There could be a bug in the program, but in most cases the fault is due to a file being damaged or accidentally removed. Reinstalling the program over the original installation will often repair the damage. The uninstaller for the program might include a repair option. If that does not have the desired effect, try uninstalling the program, shutting down the computer, rebooting it, and then installing the application again. There is probably a bug in the program if neither method of reinstallation cures the problem. It is then a matter of contacting the program's manufacturer to see if a software fix is available.

Failed test

If the test page is not produced properly, it is likely that the printer driver is not installed properly, or that there is some other Windows related problem. You can try getting Windows to find a solution to the problem by going to the Devices and Printers window, right-clicking the printer's icon, and selecting the Troubleshoot option from the pop-up menu. To some extent Windows troubleshooters try to locate problems by making their own investigations, but they often rely quite heavily on input from the user via a series of simple questionnaires. Hopefully, this approach results in the nature of the problem being gradually narrowed down until the exact problem is discovered.

A more direct method is likely to be quicker if the problem is due to a faulty or incorrectly installed driver. The simplest approach is to uninstall the printer and then reinstall it from scratch. It can be uninstalled by right-clicking its icon in the Devices and Printers window, and selecting the Remove device option from the pop-up menu. As always with this type of thing, you will have to confirm that you really do wish to go ahead and remove the printer before Windows will actually go ahead and do so. With the printer removed from Windows, it is best to shut down the computer and then try installing the printer again, being careful to do so exactly in accordance with the manufacturer's instructions.

It is not exactly rare for the computer hardware manufacturers to produce updates to the driver software for their products. In fact it seems to be the norm with some of the more complex components such as video cards. Some of the updates add functionality or make improvements to the performance of the hardware, but most of them are needed to remove bugs or resolve conflicts with other items of hardware.

Windows has a facility for adding a new printer driver, and it is accessed by right-clicking the printer's icon in the Devices and Printers window, and then selecting the Properties option from the pop-up menu. This brings up the Properties window for the printer (Figure 2.6), and there is a New Driver button in the section under the Advanced tab. Operating this button starts the Add Printer Driver Wizard (Figure 2.7), and it is then just a matter of going through each step until the Wizard has all the information it requires.

However, this Wizard is not necessarily the right way of updating an old driver or adding a new one. The hardware manufacturers tend to have their own ways of doing things, and in many cases their driver software can only be installed properly if it is handled using the method described in their installation instructions. The manufacturer's installation instructions should therefore be followed "to the letter" even if they are at odds with the standard Windows way of doing things. Driver software often comes in the form of an installation program and some supporting files. You might have to do nothing more than run the program and agree to the licence conditions. The installation program does everything else.

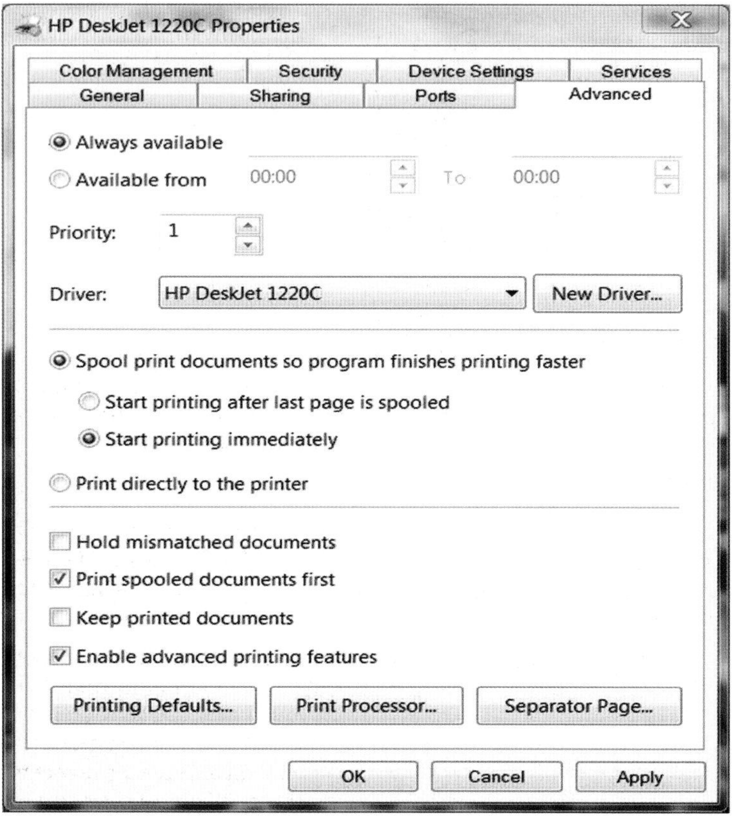

Fig.2.6 The Properties window for the printer

Self test

Many printers have a built-in testing facility that prints a test page when a certain combination of control buttons is pressed, or when the appropriate menu item is selected. Where appropriate, the printer's instruction manual will give details of how to produce the test page, and it will also show what the correctly printed page should look like. This method of testing is different to getting Windows to produce a test page. The Windows method checks the printer divers, the printer port, the connecting cable, and the printer itself. The entire system is functioning correctly if the test page is printed correctly, and the fault must then be in the applications software.

The built-in test page is stored in a memory chip inside the printer, and a correctly printed page shows that the printer is largely operational. However, this type of checking does not involve the PC or the connecting cable, and the test page will normally be produced even if the printer is not connected to a computer. A correctly produced test page

Fig.2.7 The Add Printer Driver Wizard

then probably means that the problem lies in the computer or the data cable, but it is important to realise that this type of testing does not involve the input port of the printer. Consequently, there could be a fault in the printer's interface circuitry.

If the whole system seems to be free from faults, the self-testing procedure produces the correct result, but it is still not possible to print from Windows, a fault in the printer's interface is the most likely cause of the problem. Ideally, the printer should be tried with another computer and data lead. A lack of response when the printer is driven from the computer almost certainly means that the interface circuitry is faulty. Perfect results using the new cable and computer probably indicates a fault in the original data lead or the first PC's port hardware. Try the printer with the first computer again, but this time use the second printer cable. The original printer cable is faulty if this clears the problem, and the port hardware is faulty if the problem persists.

Slow printing

The print quality produced by computer printers has improved immensely over the years, but the speed at which printers output completed pages has not really changed very much. The dot-matrix printers I used in the early days of home computing were limited to low quality monochrome text and graphics, but they could print a page of text more quickly than the printers I own today! Then, as now, few printers actually managed to reach the speeds claimed in the advertising literature.

Many users suspect that there is a fault with their printer because it fails to meet the printing speeds quoted by the manufacturer. When looking at printing speeds it has to be borne in mind that these usually assume ideal operating conditions, which might be difficult to reproduce in practice. In fact, independent tests on printers often fail to get close to the quoted printing speeds. Therefore, the figures quoted by manufacturers have to be taken with the proverbial "pinch of salt".

Also, bear in mind that printing speeds are usually dependent on the type of printing that is undertaken. The obvious example is the difference in print speeds of a typical inkjet printer when used for monochrome text printing and colour photographs. An inkjet printer might produce a few pages per minute when printing text, even if used in the highest quality mode. Printing large colour photographs is likely to reduce the print speed to so many minutes per page rather than so many pages per minute. Many inkjet printers take 10 to 20 minutes to produce full-page colour photographs at the highest quality setting.

The file format also seems to have some influence on printing speeds, particularly when using a printer that relies on Windows and the computer to do most of the processing. The Adobe PDF (Portable Document Format) is one that seems to make most printers grind along at a much slower rate than normal. One reason for this is probably that PDF tends to be used for complex pages containing a mixture of text and graphics, which is a combination that often produces relatively slow printing speeds.

Anyway, it certainly takes a large amount of processing to turn PDF files into printed documents, and most printers do the job more quickly if they are driven from a powerful computer equipped with plenty of memory. With any complex pages there is a risk that the printing speed will be limited by the speed of the PC rather than the physical limits of the printer, especially when using an old PC equipped with a relatively small amount of memory.

When printing colour photographs it is worth experimenting with the various quality settings to determine which one is best for your purposes. Sometimes there is a choice between two high quality modes that provide much the same print quality with most types of printing paper. There is no point in using the highest quality mode if it takes five times as long to print each photograph and the results do not look significantly better than when using a supposedly lower quality mode.

Streaky printing

Laser printers sometimes produce pages that contain pale vertical streaks that run the full height of the printed part of the page. This effect tends to be more noticeable on photographs than on text, but it gradually becomes worse until it is obvious on any page content. The usual cause is that the toner powder is not evenly distributed across the full width of the paper. There should be no problem initially provided you follow the manufacturer's installation instructions, and gently shake the cartridge backward and forward a number of times before fitting it in the printer. This distributes the toner reasonably evenly, and with a lot of toner present in the cartridge there should be no faint areas on the printed pages.

As the toner is used up, it is inevitable that streaky printing will eventually occur. Any parts of the cartridge where the toner is a bit shallow at first will start to run out of toner first. The toner will be used quite quickly in some parts of the cartridge while other parts will have a much lower rate of consumption. As parts of the cartridge start to run out of toner powder, the streaks start to reappear on the corresponding parts of the printed pages.

Most printer manufacturers recommend that the toner cartridge be replaced when the streaking starts to appear. However, there is usually a fair amount of toner left in the cartridge, which can therefore be given a new lease of life by repeating the shaking treatment. With one of the smaller personal laser printers, there is no need to remove the cartridge. The whole printer can be shaken backward and forward. This is clearly impractical with anything other than the smallest laser printers, and in most cases the cartridge will have to be removed, shaken and then refitted. A surprising number of additional pages can often be squeezed out of a cartridge using this simple process, particularly when the toner was not evenly distributed in the first place. In addition to saving money, this is also the "green" thing to do.

The shaking can be repeated when the streaky pages start to appear a second time, but there is a limit to the number of times that this process will work. It becomes more difficult to spread out the powder as the amount in the cartridge reduces. Eventually there will be an insufficient quantity to produced good quality printouts, and the cartridge will then have to be replaced or refilled.

Colour problems

Undoubtedly the most common printing problem I am asked to sort out is inkjet printers that produce totally inaccurate colours. In most cases there is no fault at all, and it is just that one of the ink reservoirs has run out. Inkjet printers operate on a four-colour system known as CMYK (cyan, magenta, yellow, and black). Cyan, magenta, and yellow are the three primary colours, and they are mixed to produce all the other colours. Black is added to give darker colours, and less ink is used to give paler colours. The paper, which must be white in order to produce the correct colours, effectively adds the white that gives the pale colours.

The black ink is used for printing text, and this type of printing will not be possible if the black cartridge runs out of ink. Colour printing will still be possible, but without the black ink there will be no dark colours. Black and white text printing can proceed normally when the colour cartridge has run out of ink, as can the printing of monochrome images. However, colour printing will produce some odd looking results.

One of the three coloured inks will run out before the other two reservoirs run dry, and this will affect any colours that require the missing primary colour. This can leave some parts of a colour photograph looking remarkable normal, while other areas are heavily affected. Up-market inkjet printers sometimes use more than three colours in an attempt to obtain greater colour accuracy, and the result of one colour running dry is then less drastic. It will still produce very noticeable errors in the colours though.

Where the problem is due to an exhausted ink cartridge, replacing it should cure the problem. If a new cartridge does not make any difference, then one of the tubes connecting the ink cartridge to the print head has become blocked, or part of the print head has become clogged. Either way, the printer needs to be professionally serviced. Some printers, including all the Hewlett Packard DeskJet printers, have the print head built into the ink cartridge. This method has its detractors, but it has the big advantage that you get a new print head when you fit a new cartridge. Fitting a new cartridge therefore cures any ink blockage problems.

A major repair on an inkjet printer often costs more than the value of the printer. It is then more economic to buy a new printer rather than have the old one repaired. There are kits available that can be used to clean the ink paths when a blockage occurs, and it might be worthwhile trying one of these before discarding a printer that is otherwise in good condition. A few printers have print heads that can be replaced by the user, but this is by no means the norm. Also, the cost of a replacement print head is likely to be quite high.

Stripy printing

Printouts having horizontal stripes are a common problem with inkjet printers. Most printers of this type require a calibration process to be carried out before they are used, and many need this process to be repeated each time that a new ink cartridge is fitted. These stripes are very likely to occur if the calibration is omitted or not carried out properly. It is possible for a printer to creep out of calibration, so it is worth repeating this process if the stripes start to emerge when the printer has been in use for some time.

Thin white stripes across the pages normally indicate that some of the nozzles in the print head are not firing ink droplets. In most cases this occurs because the ink cartridge is nearing exhaustion. It is unfortunate if replacing the cartridge does not cure the fault, because this means that the nozzles are blocked and an expensive repair is needed, or a new printer.

Spotty printing

When an inkjet printer produces printouts that contain random spots of ink, it is usually the result of an earlier paper jam or other fault that resulted in ink from the print head getting into the paper feed mechanism. The easiest way of clearing away the ink is to repeatedly feed a sheet of paper through the printer. It should gradually mop up the ink and restore clean printouts. If the spotting occurs when there has been no previous mishap, check that the cartridge is installed properly. Any ink in the cartridge compartment should be mopped up, and the ink cartridge must be replaced if the problem persists.

The problem might simply be due to an excessive flow of ink. With printers that have the print head and ink reservoirs combined, this problem should be cured by replacing the ink cartridge. An expensive repair might be needed if the cartridge and print head are separate units, or it might be time to buy a new printer. However, before seeking a repair or a replacement printer, make sure that you are using a suitable type of paper, and that the printer is set for use with that type of paper. Some types of paper require relatively little ink, and will often produce spotty and smudgy results if the printer is set for use with the wrong type of paper.

Laser printers can also have problems with spotty printouts, but the same pattern of dots usually appears on every page. Typically, the spots appear slightly lower on successive pages, eventually moving back to the top again. Looking at things in highly simplified terms, the electrostatic image is normally "drawn" onto plastic film by the laser beam, and then transferred to the paper. The toner powder is then attracted to the appropriate parts of the paper and heated so that it melts and glues itself in place. When dust finds its way onto the plastic film it upsets the normal operation of the printer and tends to produce corresponding specks on the printouts.

With some laser printers the photosensitive drum is not a consumable and it cannot be replaced easily. The cost of repair is usually very much more than the value of the printer. Fortunately, this type of printer seems to be largely immune to the dust problem. Realistically, if it should occur there are only two options available. Put up with it or buy a new laser printer. Many laser printers do have a user changeable drum, but the replaceable type is not necessarily very drum-like. In catalogues it is usually called something like a "photo-conductor". With a photo-conductor that is well used, the obvious solution is to replace it. As these units are quite expensive, you may well be reluctant to replace one that has received relatively little use. Depending on the design of the printer, it is sometimes possible to remove the photo-conductor, clean it, and then refit it in the printer. The cleaning has to be done carefully though, as it is easy to add more dust than you remove. Lens cleaning kits for cameras are useful for this job.

Wireless peripherals

Devices that connect to the computer without using any connecting wires fall into two general types, which are the Bluetooth devices and the rest. Here we will mainly be considering simple wireless gadgets such as mice and keyboards that are not usually of the Bluetooth variety. However, some of the areas covered are general in nature, and are applicable to any wireless peripheral.

Wireless computer gadgets have a transmitter in the peripheral itself, and a receiver unit that plugs into the computer via what will normally be a USB port. The receiver will be powered from the USB port and is unlikely to require much power or very high speed operation. It should therefore work with any normal USB port, but might give difficulties if used with a passive hub that has numerous USB ports. Unlike normal mice, keyboards, etc., the wireless type need a built-in power source, because there is no way of obtaining power from the computer. The built-in power source provides power for the device itself and for the transmitter.

Power is normally provided by an ordinary battery pack such as a couple of normal AAA cells, but some wireless gadgets have built-in rechargeable batteries. Rechargeable batteries are normally supplied in an uncharged state, so new wireless gadgets of this type are unusable until they have been at least partially recharged. Batteries are sometimes included with gadgets that use ordinary AA or AAA cells, but there can be a gap of months or even years between the equipment leaving the factory and someone actually buying it. The batteries may well have become flat due to ageing during this time. If a new wireless device fails to work, then recharging or replacing the batteries, as appropriate, is the first thing to try.

If a wireless device has been working normally for some time but starts to give problems it is again problems with the batteries that should be checked first. Some wireless devices use up batteries at quite a high rate, so new batteries might be required even if they were replaced not that long ago. In the same way that paper tends to be a weak point with printers, batteries tend to be a weakness of many modern electronic gadgets.

Sometimes the batteries seem to run down at a rate that makes running costs quite high, but the batteries have not actually gone flat at all. It is simply that the battery contacts have become a bit corroded and that this prevents a good electrical connection from being made. This is certainly the case if removing the batteries and reinstalling the same ones cures the problem. Taking the batteries out and then fitting them again cleans the contacts and restores normal operation for a while. Using a clean cloth to rub the contacts on the batteries themselves and the ones in the gadget should provide a cure that lasts much longer than just removing and refitting the batteries.

Drivers

If a wireless gadget seems to be working, with various indicator lights operating in the appropriate fashion, but it is ignored by Windows, the most likely cause of the problem is that the driver software has not been installed properly, or at all. With any PC peripheral device it is important to remember that it is not just a matter of having it connected to the computer correctly. The device will be ignored by the operating system and all application programs unless the correct driver software is properly installed in Windows.

Many of the more simple peripheral gadgets, and some of the more complex ones come to that, are of the so-called "Plug-and-Play" variety.

In order to use "Plug-and-Play" devices it is just a matter of plugging them into a USB socket. They are then detected by Windows which automatically installs the correct driver software. There will be a delay of several seconds while this software is installed, but the device is then ready for use. Wireless gadgets, even if they are fairly basic items of hardware such as keyboards or mice, will not necessarily be true "Plug-and-Play" devices. They really require two sets of drivers, which are one for the wireless interface and one for the device itself. In order to avoid problems you should always read the manufacturer's installation instructions and follow them "to the letter".

Making waves

Using a couple of wireless devices such as a keyboard and mouse will not usually cause any problems, especially in cases where they are sold together as a set. However, there can be problems if further wireless gadgets are added, and this is simply due to them working on the same or very similar frequencies so that they tend to jam each others' signals. It is therefore best not to get carried away with wireless devices and to keep things within reason.

Wireless devices are not limited to line of sight operation, but this is not to say that the signal cannot be blocked by objects getting in the way. There is also a phenomenon called "standing waves" which can produce "dead" areas with no signal. This effect is produced by a reflected radio signal that cancels out the direct signal, effectively giving little or no signal. The practical consequence of all this is that you can sometimes find that there are places where wireless devices do not work well or fail to work at all, even though they work perfectly practically anywhere else in the room. Sometimes it is possible to make a "dead" area usable by moving the receiver unit slightly, connecting it to the computer via a short USB extension lead if necessary.

Reconnecting

Some wireless devices are not good at re-establishing contact with the receiver unit if the signal is briefly interrupted for some reason. Regaining the connection might require nothing more than briefly placing the wireless device very close to the receiver. Another ploy that will sometimes work is to switch off the wireless gadget, wait a few seconds, and then switch it on again. Some wireless equipment has a reset switch or switches. The instruction manual should then give the correct procedure for re-establishing contact between the two units.

Laptops and notebooks

Bad old days

At one time you would only buy a portable PC such as a laptop or notebook if you really needed the ability to compute while on the move. The drawbacks of mobile PCs were many, while the advantages were few. In fact there was probably only one significant advantage, which was the ability to work away from a mains power point. Even this advantage was not all it could be. The battery life of portable PCs tended to be very limited, and even if a spare battery was carried you soon needed a mains supply.

Apart from their portability, laptop and notebook PCs tended to compare very unfavourably with desktop PCs. Many of the drawbacks centred on the usability of portable PCs, or perhaps it would be more accurate to say their lack of usability. One of the main points of contention was the poor screens fitted to most of the devices. Most had monochrome screens that were all right for basic business applications such as spread sheets and word processing, but were of little use for things such as photo editing and most graphics applications. The lack of colour could still be something of a drawback in the more simple applications, and it was certainly a very undesirable feature. Colour screens were actually available quite early in the development of portable PCs, but at a price. That price was often so high that only the "well heeled" amongst us could seriously consider buying one.

Whether a colour or monochrome screen was chosen, its performance was likely to be quite poor in most respects. The LCD screen technology meant that everything was very precise, but a lack of contrast often gave the perception of a rather fuzzy picture that lacked detail. The screens were small and often operated at relatively low resolutions, which added to the impression of fuzziness and lack of detail. The main complaint of most users seemed to be the very narrow viewing angles of these early

LCD screens. In order to get the best results from these screens they had to be viewed from directly in front. The brightness dropped dramatically if you moved slightly out of position. With some screens it looked as if the computer had been switched off if you moved your head slightly to one side! Another problem was that the screens were relatively dim even when viewed from the correct position.

There were other problems such as poor quality keyboards, and a lack of battery life, but probably the main one was a general lack of performance. You tended to pay the price of an upmarket desktop PC for a portable PC that would struggle to keep up with the cheapest desktop computer. It was not that your expensive laptop computer would not run the latest "shoot-em-up" action games, it would probably struggle with less demanding programs as well.

Things move on in the world in general and in the sphere of computing, and this has resulted in portable PCs becoming more competitive with desktop PCs. Many people now buy portable PCs even though they will not need to do any computing on the move. It is probably still the case that a typical desktop PC is significantly faster than a typical laptop, but a modern laptop is fast enough to handle most everyday applications. The screen of a laptop PC is generally smaller than that of a desktop PC, but they are still perfectly adequate in this respect. Lack of battery life is still a problem, but this obviously does not apply if a laptop PC will mainly be used at home.

There are two huge advantages of portable PCs that probably account for their huge increase in popularity. I suspect that the main reason for their massive rise in popularity is that they require less space. The manufacturers of electrical and electronic goods seem to come up with an endless stream of new gadgets. Modern life is incomplete unless you obtain practically all of these must-have devices. Unfortunately, the rooms in our houses do not expand slightly each time a new gadget comes along! You can use a laptop PC on the kitchen table or literally on your lap, and having completed your tasks it can then be stored in a cupboard or drawer.

On the cheap

The other major advantage of a laptop computer is the relatively low running costs. The cost of running a PC has steadily increased over the years, with electricity tending to become much more expensive, and computers becoming bigger, better and more power "thirsty". The power consumption of a modern desktop PC can easily be 300 to 400 watts, or even more. Modern LCD monitors use less power than the old CRT variety, but they can still add a further 100 watts to the total power consumption. This makes running costs quite high even for those using a PC an hour or two per day. It makes the running costs very high for those that use a PC all day and practically every day.

In order to obtain a reasonable battery life it is necessary for a portable PC to have a very low level of power consumption by normal PC standards. The lower the rate at which power is drained from the computer's battery, the less likely you are to find that the battery has gone flat before you have completed the current task! The actual power consumption seems to vary greatly from one laptop to another, but something like 50 to 65 watts seems to be typical.

Bear in mind that this is the consumption of the entire computer, including the monitor. It is therefore around one fifth to one tenth of the power consumption of a typical desktop PC and LCD monitor. You could run a laptop PC all day and all night on little more than a single unit of electricity. Over a period of a few years the saving in running costs obtained by using a laptop PC instead of a desktop type could easily be several hundred pounds. In fact the saving could be greater than the cost of the computer. This is something that should definitely be borne in mind if you do a great deal of computing on a tight budget.

Screen resolution

With any new PC, laptop or otherwise, in theory it is ready for use after any final installation processes have been completed. In the real world it is usually necessary to do a certain amount of customising and install some software before a new PC is ready to be used in earnest. As supplied, the computer should have video settings that give good results with Windows itself, and with most application programs. The screen settings will usually have the monitor operating at its native resolution, which is the resolution that will give optimum results in most situations. However, under certain circumstances it can be advantageous to alter the video settings, including the resolution used.

For example, some games might not work very well with default settings. The specifications of modern laptop computers are quite good, but in general they still have less computing power than desktop PCs. Changing to a lower resolution and fewer colours will often give faster and smoother action, albeit with lower quality graphics. This is simply because a

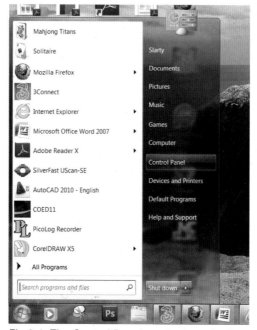

Fig.3.1 The Control Panel can be launched from the Start menu

reduction in resolution and colours reduces the loading on the computer's microprocessor and graphics circuits. There are other occasions when a change in the video settings could be advantageous, such as when using the computer with an external monitor.

When you need to change the video settings, the first task is to launch the Windows Control Panel. The available routes to this built-in Windows program depend on how Windows is set up, but with a new installation there should be a menu entry for it in the Start menu (Figure 3.1). Left-click the Start button in the bottom left-hand corner of the Windows Desktop, and then left-click the Control Panel entry. A new window containing the Control Panel should then appear (Figure 3.2).

Next, left-click the "Adjust screen resolution" link in the Appearance and Personalization section of the Control Panel. This will change the window to look like Figure 3.3. Here there is a menu that allows the screen resolution to be altered, although the drop-down menu will probably be in the form of a fancy slider control. The screen resolution control can be used to alter the horizontal and vertical resolution of the screen, and there will typically be about half a dozen combinations on offer.

A computer's display is produced from thousands of tiny dots, or pixels as they are called. It is a sort of high-tech mosaic. Screen resolution is specified in terms of the number of pixels used. With a screen resolution of (say) 1024 by 768, there are 1024 pixels in each row, and 768 rows.

Fig.3.2 The normal version of the Windows Control Panel

This gives 786,432 pixels in total, which might sound a lot, but this is about the minimum that will give good results with much of the software in use today.

Ideal resolution

Opinions differ about the ideal screen resolution, but it is dependent on the type of software you will be running and the characteristics of the monitor you are using. In general, higher resolution is better, but only if your monitor can handle it properly. In the case of a laptop, its LCD screen should give good results at its highest resolution. However, high resolution requires a large monitor so that you can see everything clearly. Even for those with good eyesight, a small but highly detailed screen is difficult to use. Using a PC is likely to be very tiring if you have to strain your eyesight in order to see the screen properly. It could be harmful to your eyesight as well. A laptop that has a small screen which normally runs at a high resolution might be easier to use if a lower resolution is selected.

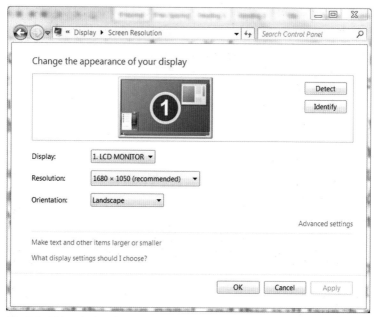

Fig.3.3 This window has a menu that can be used to alter the screen resolution

This is really a subjective matter, and you have to choose whatever resolution suits you best. If you are happy with the default setting of the highest resolution then there is probably nothing to be gained by altering this setting. It is clearly worth trying some alternatives if you find some parts of the screen hard to see properly. There will not necessarily be one setting that is ideal for all applications. You might find that it is better to use (say) the highest resolution most of the time, but to switch to a lower resolution when going online and using the Internet.

Further adjustments can be made by operating the Advanced Settings link in the middle section of the Screen Resolution window. This brings up a new window where the Monitor tab should be selected (Figure 3.4). The Colors menu near the bottom of the window will probably have 32-bit operation selected by default. Using Windows 7 it is likely that the only other option will be 16-bit operation, although there might also be a 24-bit option. Selecting 16-bit operation might help to slightly speed up a PC that has sluggish graphics performance, and it is unlikely to give a noticeable reduction in the picture quality. This setting controls the maximum number of different colours that can be displayed, and 16-bit

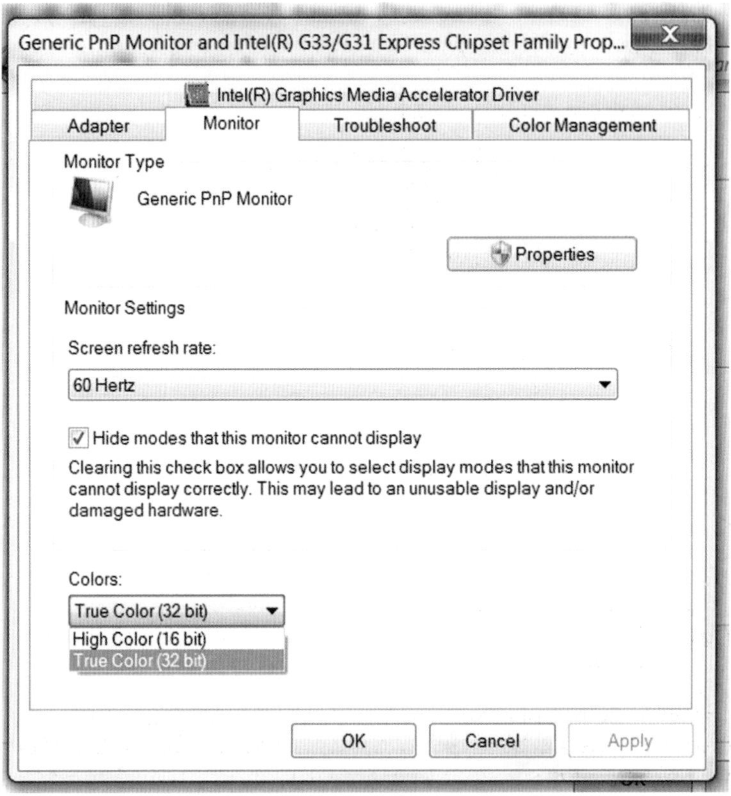

Fig.3.4 The colour depth can be changed via this window

operation gives a range of over 65 thousand colours, which is more than adequate for most purposes.

The scan rate used by the monitor used to be an important factor. In the past it was quite common for monitors to have impressive maximum resolutions, but these could only be achieved by resorting to quite low scan rates with the picture being updated at around 25 to 35 times per second. This usually gave a picture that had a noticeable flickering, making these monitors difficult to use for anything other than short periods. There should be no problem with screen flicker when using the built-in LCD monitor of a laptop PC. It could be a significant factor if the laptop is connected to an external monitor, but these days it is unlikely that you will ever find it necessary to alter the "Screen refresh rate" setting.

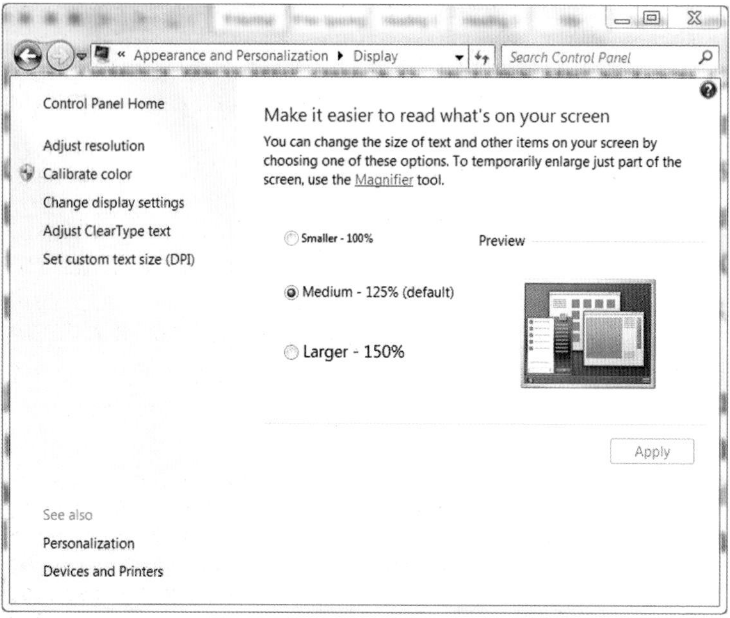

Fig.3.5 A smaller or larger text size can be selected here

A slight problem with some flat panel monitors is that they do not handle fast movement very well. For example, an onscreen object moving quickly across the screen can tend to leave a slight and brief trail. With many types of software this is not particularly noticeable, but it can very apparent with some games or when playing videos on a PC. This is just a characteristic of some monitors and there is nothing that can be done about it by adjusting the video settings. Fortunately this aspect of monitor design has improved enormously in recent years, and you are unlikely to encounter major problems with screen trails.

Larger text

As pointed out previously, there is a potential problem when changing to a different screen resolution, which is simply that a resolution that works well in one application, will not necessarily work well in others. Some programs might be easier to use with reduced resolution, while others will not run at reduced screen resolutions. This can result in frequent changes, which can become a bit tedious after a while.

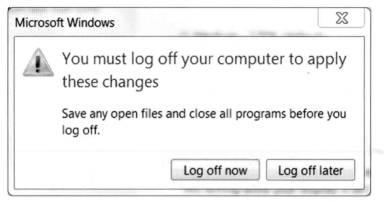

Fig.3.6 The changes will not take effect until you log off and on again

An alternative approach to the problem is to increase the size of text and certain other on-screen objects such as icons. In the Control Panel window of Figure 3.3 there is a "Make text and other items larger or smaller" link, and activating this brings up the window of Figure 3.5. The computer should become easier to use if you leave the screen resolution at its maximum but select the Larger option in Figure 3.5. Selecting this produces the small window of Figure 3.6. You can opt to log off immediately provided there are no application programs running.

This takes you to the log on screen where the icon for the appropriate user should be left-clicked. In most cases there will only be one user, and it is then just a matter of left-clicking the single icon in the centre of the screen. Logging on takes you to the Windows desktop, and any icons present there should be noticeably larger than before. It is best to choose the "Log off later" option if you have application programs running when the window of Figure 3.6 appears. This avoids the risk of losing any work carried out recently using the application programs. The changes will take effect the next time you log off and on again, or the next time you boot into Windows. As before, any icons on the desktop should be much larger than before.

Figures 3.7 and 3.8 show a document loaded into Microsoft's Word program with the text at the Large and Medium settings respectively. The icons and so on at the top of the screen are noticeably larger in Figure 3.7. For those with something less than normal eyesight, and particularly for those who are longsighted, this should make the program easier to use. The downside is that the toolbars, etc., at the top of the

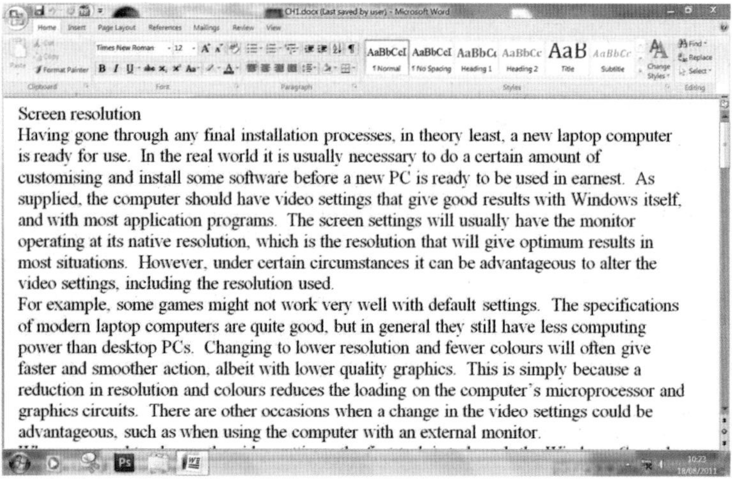

Fig.3.7 Using a larger text size has made the text in the toolbars larger

screen occupy more of the screen, leaving less space to display the document. However, in most cases the reduction in the work area is unlikely to be of any real consequence.

It might seem strange that the loaded text is exactly the same size in Figures 3.7 and 3.8, but this is due to the fact that the size of displayed text in many application programs is controlled by the program settings and not by the Windows operating system. In most cases the default text setting will be larger if you switch to the Larger text option, but within an application program the text size can still be controlled in the normal way. In these examples, the text is at the setting that makes it fill the screen from side to side.

Deleting

Laptop computers, and most other types come to that, tend to be supplied with some preinstalled software. Some of the programs might be fully working and of real use to you, but much of it is likely to be demonstration software that is either something less than fully functioning, or will only run for (typically) one month. It then ceases to work unless you pay a registration fee. Some of the fully operational software might be of no interest to you, and might actually be a bit of a nuisance. You might find that aptly named "nag screens" keep appearing, extolling the virtues of

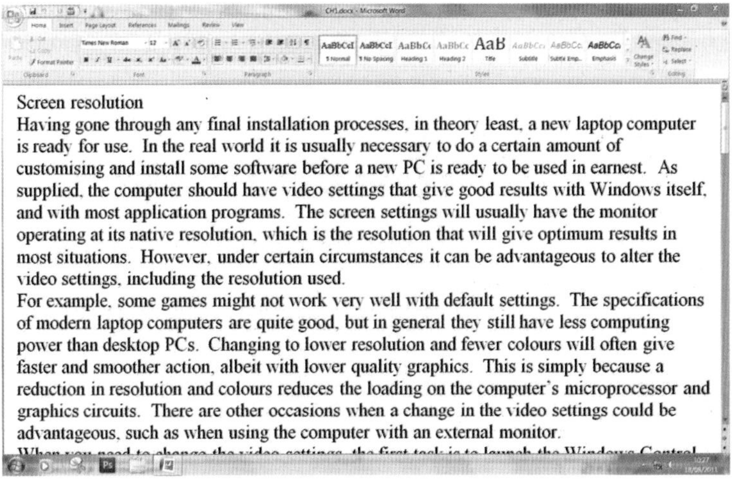
Screen resolution
Having gone through any final installation processes, in theory least, a new laptop computer is ready for use. In the real world it is usually necessary to do a certain amount of customising and install some software before a new PC is ready to be used in earnest. As supplied, the computer should have video settings that give good results with Windows itself, and with most application programs. The screen settings will usually have the monitor operating at its native resolution, which is the resolution that will give optimum results in most situations. However, under certain circumstances it can be advantageous to alter the video settings, including the resolution used.
For example, some games might not work very well with default settings. The specifications of modern laptop computers are quite good, but in general they still have less computing power than desktop PCs. Changing to lower resolution and fewer colours will often give faster and smoother action, albeit with lower quality graphics. This is simply because a reduction in resolution and colours reduces the loading on the computer's microprocessor and graphics circuits. There are other occasions when a change in the video settings could be advantageous, such as when using the computer with an external monitor.

Fig.3.8 This is the same as Fig.3.7, but using the normal text size

the deluxe version of the program which can be obtained for a suitable registration fee.

It is advisable to uninstall any unused software which will otherwise use up hard disc space and could also make unfruitful use of other aspects of the computer's resources. Removing unwanted software from a PC is not usually too difficult, but it is important to go about things in the right fashion. Simply deleting the files and folders associated with programs you wish to remove is definitely going about things in the wrong fashion. It will certainly free some hard disc space, but deleting program files and folders is also likely to produce a few problems.

Most programs are installed onto the computer using an installation program, and this program does not simply make folders on the hard disc and copy files into them from the CD-ROM. It will also make changes to the Windows configuration files so that the program is properly integrated with the operating system. If you simply delete the program's directory structure to get rid of it, Windows will not be aware that the program has been removed. During the boot-up process the operating system will probably look for files associated with the deleted program, and will produce error messages when it fails to find them.

Matters are actually more involved than this, and there is another potential problem in that Windows utilizes shared files. This is where one file, such as a DLL type, is shared by two or more programs. In deleting a

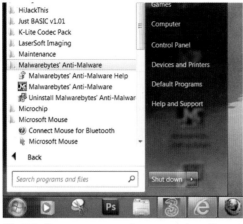

Fig.3.9 Some programs have an uninstaller

program and the other files in its directory structure you could also be deleting files needed by other programs. This could prevent other programs from working properly, or even from starting up at all. If a program is loaded onto the hard disc using an installation program, the only safe way of removing it is to use an uninstaller program.

Custom uninstaller

Some programs load an uninstaller program onto the hard disc as part of the installation process. The uninstaller is then available via the Start menu if you choose All Programs, and then the name of the program concerned. This only applies where the entry in the menu has the yellow folder icon. When you choose this option there will be the program itself plus at least one additional option in the sub-menu that appears. If there is no uninstall option here, no custom uninstaller has been installed for that program. The example of Figure 3.9 shows the submenu for the Malwarebytes anti-malware security program, and this one does include an option to uninstall the program. Uninstaller programs of this type are almost invariably automatic in operation, so you have to do little more than instruct it to go ahead with the removal of the program.

With any uninstaller software you may be asked if certain files should be removed. This mostly occurs where the program finds shared files that no longer appear to be shared. In days gone by it did not seem to matter whether you opted to remove or leave these files, with Windows always failing to work properly thereafter! These days things seem to be more reliable, and it is reasonably safe to accept either option. To leave the files in place is certainly the safest option, but it also results in files and possibly folders being left on the disc unnecessarily.

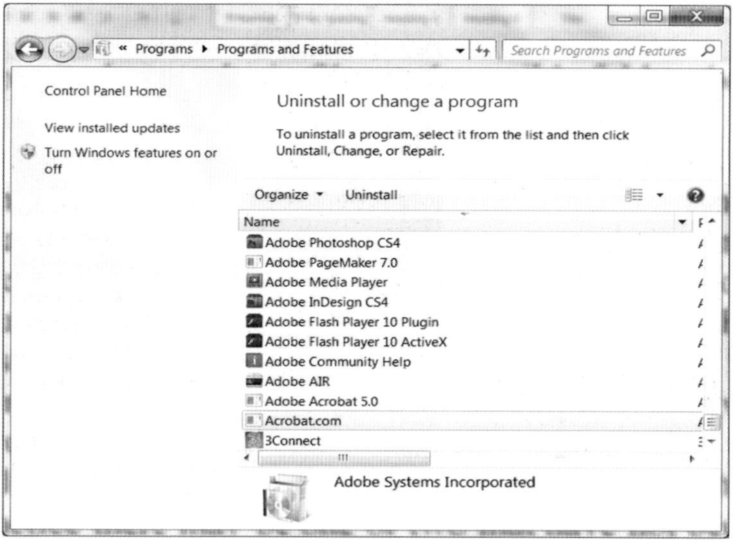

Fig.3.10 All the installed programs will be listed here

Windows uninstaller

Windows has a built-in uninstaller that can be accessed via the control panel. From the Start menu select Control Panel, and then left-click the "Uninstall a program" link in the Programs section. This takes you to the uninstaller, and the main section of the screen shows a list of the programs that can be uninstalled via this route (Figure 3.10). Removing a program is just a matter of selecting it from the list by left-clicking its entry, and then operating the Uninstall or Uninstall/Remove button near the top of the window. Confirm that you wish to remove the program when prompted in the new window that appears, and the removal process will then begin. With some programs you might be offered several options such as repairing or installing more components, and in this case it is the Remove or Uninstall option that should be taken. Then, as before, confirm that you wish to remove the program.

Ease of Access Center

Windows has some built-in facilities that are intended to make the computer easier to use, particularly for those of us with eyesight that is

Fig.3.11 Launch the Ease of Access Center

less than perfect. These facilities can be accessed via the Ease of Access Center, which is available by going to Start menu, selecting All Programs, then Accessories, Ease of Access, and Ease of Access Center (Figure 3.11). Once launched (Figure 3.12), the Ease of Access Center has links that enable four utility programs to be launched. It is worth noting that the four main programs of the Ease of Access Center can also be accessed directly via the Ease of Access submenu.

It is worth trying the Magnifier program, which provides a magnified view of the area around the pointer or cursor (Figure 3.13). In addition to the window that shows the magnified view, a small control panel is launched when the Magnifier program is run (Figure 3.14). This enables two aspects of the magnified view to be controlled, such as the degree of magnification, and whether the normal (Lens) mode is used, or the magnifier window is docked. In the docked setting the magnifier window does not follow the cursor around the screen, but instead stays in the same place (Figure 3.15). The position of the magnified view on the screen can be altered by dragging and resizing the window in normal Windows fashion.

The magnifier is included primarily as a means of reading small text more easily, but it will magnify any area of the screen, whether it contains text or graphics, as demonstrated by the two examples provided here in Figure 3.13 and 3.15. The Magnifier program seems to work better with some computers that it does with others, and the pointer can become a bit flashy and intermittent when this program is running. As with many programs, it probably runs more smoothly with a computer that has a fast processor and video section. It is certainly worth trying though, and there are more sophisticated commercial magnifier programs available if you need something better.

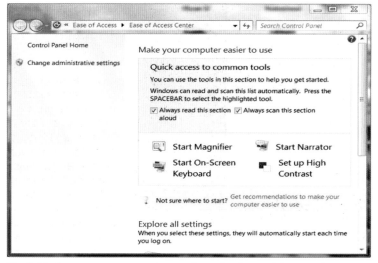

Fig.3.12 Four programs can be run from the Ease of Access Center

All talk

Taking things a stage further, you can try the Narrator program. This can be set up in various ways, but its basic action is to describe the buttons, etc., in the current window, and to read text. It can also tell you which keys you are operating when using the keyboard. The ability of the program to read blocks of text is probably the one that is of most general use. Rather than straining your eyes or using the Magnifier program to make reading text easier, you simply have the Narrator program read it to you via the computer's audio system.

It does not work with most text on web pages, but it is possible to use the Windows Copy and Paste facilities to transfer the text to a word processor. The built-in Wordpad program of Windows (Start – All Programs – Accessories – Wordpad) is more than adequate for this purpose. In the browser, drag the pointer through the text you wish to have read and then select Copy from the Edit menu. Then go to the word processor and select Paste from the Edit menu. If the Narrator program is running, it should then read the text, albeit with an American accent.

There are other facilities available, such as an on-screen keyboard (Figure 3.16) which can be operated using some form of pointing device. There are also facilities to set up specialised pointing devices, and to optimise

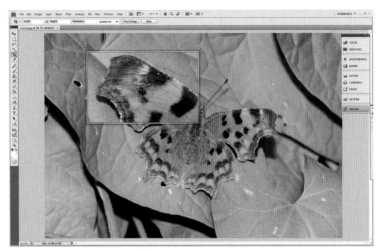

Fig.3.13 The Magnifier accessory in operation

the screen display. Obviously much of this is not of general use, but there are specialist facilities here for those who need them. The speech recognition facility enables text to be entered into a word processor by talking into a microphone rather than using the keyboard. This is something that is well worth trying if you are not skilled at using a typewriter style keyboard, but it obviously requires the computer to be equipped with a suitable microphone. Modern speech recognition systems usually achieve quite good accuracy, but they work better for some people than for others. Also, they only work well in quiet environments.

Fig.3.14 The Magnifier control panel

Battery

Problems with laptop batteries used to be quite common, but improvements in the technology have helped to make them less problematic. Even so, you would be well advised to read through the section of the manufacturer's instruction manual that deals with recharging the battery and keeping it in good condition. Some general points can be made here, but with battery technology advancing all the time it is advisable to seek specific information for the battery used in your particular laptop PC.

A common complaint with a new laptop is that the battery runs down much more quickly than expected. Apparently it is quite common for customers to return certain types of electronic gadget as faulty because they exhibit short battery lives. Portable PCs and digital cameras are the most common culprits. In most cases the devices are actually fully operational, and the short battery life is normal and not a fault!

Laptop PCs use clever techniques to keep the power consumption to a minimum, but the amount of power required to keep one operating normally is still quite high. The drain on the battery will be even higher if you undertake tasks that involve things like intensive use of the processor or continuous operation of a CD-ROM or DVD drive. The quoted operating life of the battery is typically only two or three hours, but it will be less than this if the computer is used for activities that involve relatively high levels of power consumption.

Another point to bear in mind is that some rechargeable batteries need to go through several charge/discharge cycles before they achieve full capacity. Therefore, you may need to fully charge and run down the battery a few times before it becomes fully up to standard and its operating life per charge can be assessed properly. The instruction manual should always give this recommendation in cases where the battery is a type that needs to be "exercised" before it reaches full capacity.

I generally try to take rechargeable batteries through a few charge/recharge cycles before using them in earnest regardless of whether this point is addressed by the instruction manual. In practice few rechargeable batteries seem to work really well until they have been used for a while. Another point to bear in mind is that most rechargeable batteries work best if they are run down and recharged on a

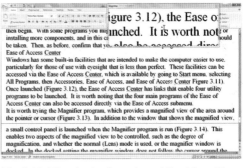

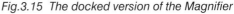

Fig.3.15 The docked version of the Magnifier

regular basis. It is likely that the battery will not perform well if it is left unused for a few weeks or more. Fortunately, in most cases it can be restored to full capacity by taking it through a full charge and discharge cycle.

Memory effect

You tend to hear a great deal about the so-called "memory effect" when rechargeable batteries are discussed. The basic premise of this is that a rechargeable battery does not provide full capacity unless it is fully discharged before it is recharged. Supposedly, recharging a 50 percent discharged battery gives you a battery of half the normal fully charged capacity. In other words, the battery "remembers" how long it was used and its state prior to being recharged, and this becomes its new capacity.

While it is true that the original nickel-cadmium (Ni-Cad) batteries work best when taken through full charge and discharge cycles, problems with the "memory effect" have perhaps been a little exaggerated at times. Fortunately, the batteries used in modern laptop PCs are not of the nickel-cadmium variety. They are mostly based on some form of lithium-iron technology, which gives higher capacities from smaller and lighter batteries. This type of battery is also totally free from any "memory effect", so there is no problem if a partially discharged battery is topped-up. Note though, that some manufacturers do recommend that the battery should occasionally be fully discharged and recharged. This will supposedly keep it in optimum condition.

Fig.3.16 The on-screen keyboard

No charge

Modern rechargeable batteries have quite long operating lives, but they do not last forever. In some instances the battery will outlast the rest of the computer, but most laptop PCs require at least one new battery during their operating life. Sometimes it is pretty obvious when the battery has failed. It does not take a significant charge and the computer either fails to switch on at all or it only does so for a few seconds before powering down again.

There will usually be some warning signs before this stage is reached. There will often be a noticeable reduction in the computing time obtained between charges. Probably the clearest sign of the impending demise of the battery is when it will not hold a charge for more than a day or two. In general, rechargeable batteries do not hold their charge as well as primary cells. Even so, they normally take a few weeks or more to fully discharge when left unused. The battery will soon need replacement if you find that it has almost fully discharged even though the computer has not been used for a few days.

Leave it in

Of course, the battery is likely to be of little interest when a laptop is used as a normal home or office PC. The computer will always be powered from the mains supply via the adaptor, rendering the battery of no use. If you will not be using the battery, should it be left in the PC or removed? There are a couple of good reasons for leaving the battery in the computer. One is simply that if you should decide to use the computer away from a mains outlet, you simply do so. The battery in the computer will be fully charged and ready for use whenever you need it. When stored outside the computer the battery will gradually lose its charge, and it will probably have to be fully recharged overnight before it can be used.

The other advantage of having the battery in the computer is that it effectively provides you with a UPS (uninterruptible power supply). The idea of a normal UPS is that it powers the computer in the event of the mains power failing. Provided everything works as it should, the batteries in the UPS take over when the mains supply fails, and the computer carries on working as if nothing had happened. A laptop computer will normally switch to battery power if the mains supply is interrupted for some reason, effectively giving it a built-in UPS. The battery will usually provide two or three hours of computing, by which time normal operation will usually have been restored.

Battery storage

If you do decide to keep the battery in the computer, it is probably as well to periodically run the battery down and recharge it again, so that it is kept in good working order. It is important to store the battery sensibly if you decide not to keep it in the computer. It should be stored in a cold dry place where there is nothing metal. Do not underestimate the amount of power that a modern laptop battery can provide. If any metal short-circuits the battery terminals it is likely that a great deal of heat will be generated. This clearly represents a fire hazard, and it will not do the battery a lot of good either.

As pointed out previously, the battery will tend to run down over a period of time even if it is not used. This means that it will have to be fully recharged before it can be used in earnest. It is a good idea to occasionally charge the battery, run it down, and recharge it again so that it is kept in good condition. If you simply leave the battery in a drawer for a few years and then try to use it, do not be surprised if it has a very limited capacity or does not work at all.

Saving power

There are ways of saving power and extending the battery life, but do not expect miracles from this type of thing. Also, there is generally a price to be paid for the reduced power consumption. This price is normally a reduction in speed at some stage of the proceedings. For example, some laptop PCs have a system that enables the computer to run at reduced power consumption, but this involves slowing down the computer for all or part of the time. The reduced speed is unlikely to be a major drawback when undertaking an undemanding task such as word processing, but it could slow down the computer to an unacceptable degree when running an application that requires a large amount of processing power.

Probably the most effective way of reducing the power consumption of the computer is to make sure that the brightness of the monitor is no higher than it really needs to be. It would be a mistake to set the brightness so low that viewing the screen is difficult. On the other hand, setting the brightness any higher than the minimum needed for comfortable viewing is just wasting power. With some laptop computers the screen brightness is automatically reduced when the battery is used as the power source. With any laptop PC there should be a control or controls specifically for setting the screen's brightness. Alternatively the keyboard and certain key combinations will give control of the screen brightness, and probably the contrast as well.

Many laptop PCs are supplied complete with a power management utility program. There are already some power management facilities available from within Windows, but these should already be at the appropriate settings for a laptop. Any supplied power management facility might be in addition to the built-in facilities of Windows, or it might replace them. Where such a utility is provided, it should have facilities that go beyond the standard ones built into Windows. With this type of thing it is necessary to carefully read through the documentation for the program to determine what features are

Fig.3.17 Laptop PCs have a built-in pointing device

available, and how they are controlled. However, do not expect adjustments to power management settings to vastly improve the battery life.

Mouse

These days all laptop computers have a built-in pointing device of some kind (Figure 3.17), but many people still use a mouse when the computer is being used at home or in the office. Some even prefer to take a mouse when using a laptop on the move. The built-in pointing devices are ingenious and have improved over the years, but few users find them genuinely easy to use. My fingers are less agile than they used to be, and I find even the better pointing devices virtually unusable. A mouse generally provides a much quicker and easier means of controlling the pointer.

Adding a mouse to a laptop PC or one of the even smaller netbook types should be very easy. Good but inexpensive USB mice are available from any computer store, and I have even seen them on sale in supermarkets. The "USB" name refers to the port on the computer that you plug the mouse into, and any reasonably modern laptop or netbook PC should have at least a couple of these ports (Figure 3.18). Note that with this type of port it is only possible to insert the plug if it is the right way up. Windows should recognise the mouse as a standard pointing device and automatically load the driver software. It can then be used just like a mouse connected to a desktop PC.

Fig.3.18 A laptop PC should have at least a couple of USB ports

A mouse is often problematic at first with the pointer either flying across the screen with the slightest of mouse movements, or a huge amount of movement is needed in order to make it move a significant distance. The ideal mouse sensitivity is very much a matter of personal preference, and it also depends to some extent on the type of software in use. High sensitivity is suitable for most programs where the pointer will only be used to make menu selections. Low sensitivity is better in situations where very precise control of the pointer is needed, which mainly means graphics applications such as photo editing and technical drawing.

Windows enables the sensitivity of the mouse to be adjusted to suit each user's requirements. The first step is to go to the Windows Control Panel. Assuming the Control Panel is in the normal Category mode, the first task is to switch it to one of the Icon modes using the drop-down menu near the top right-hand corner of the window. This gives a large list of topics, and amongst these there should be one for the mouse (Figure 3.19). The window that appears when you left-click the Mouse link depends on whether the PC is equipped with a Microsoft mouse, a generic type, or one of the more upmarket mice. In this case the mouse is a Microsoft type and it is the standard version of the Mouse Properties window that appears (Figure 3.20).

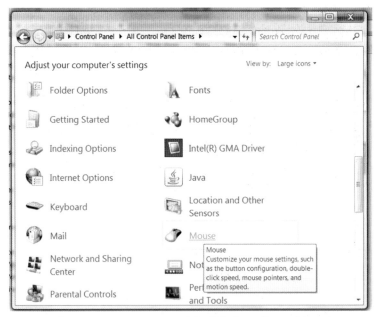

Fig.3.19 The large icons version of the Windows Control Panel

Click speed

By default it is the Buttons section that is displayed at first. This enables the functions of the mouse buttons and (where appropriate) the mouse wheel to be changed. Making changes here is unnecessary unless you find the standard arrangement awkward to use for some reason. Here it is the Activities and Pointer Options sections that are of interest, and the desired section can be displayed by left-clicking the tab of the appropriate name near the top of the window.

In the Activities section it is the slider control near the top of the window that is of interest. It enables you to adjust the maximum time that can be used between the two mouse clicks when double-clicking an onscreen object. It is likely that a slower double-click speed is required if you find that double-clicks tend to be ignored by Windows. If double-clicks are still ignored, either you are not releasing the button properly after the first mouse click, or the mouse is of low quality and it is not opening the switch contacts even though you are releasing the button sufficiently. Another possibility is that you are moving the mouse while operating the

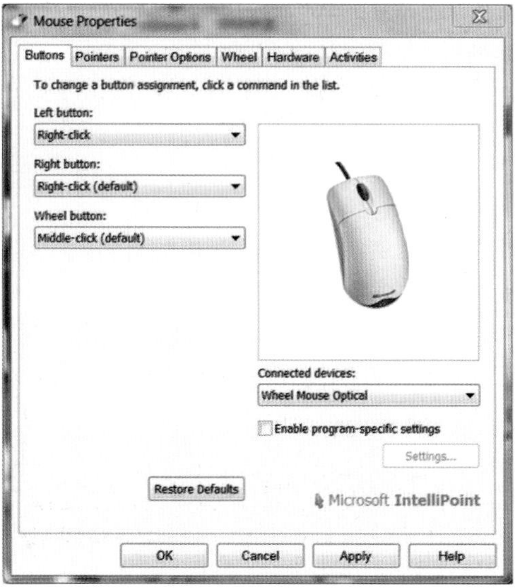

Fig.3.20 The Mouse Properties window

button. Any type of mouse clicking tends to be ignored by Windows if it occurs while the mouse and onscreen pointer are moving.

The control for the mouse sensitivity is in the Pointer Options section near the top of the window (Figure 3.21). The slider control near the top is the one that controls the sensitivity of the mouse, or the "mouse speed" in Microsoft's terminology. If the control is moved to the right a smaller amount of mouse movement will be needed in order to move the pointer a certain distance. Moving the slider to the left has the opposite effect, with greater mouse movement being needed in order to move the pointer a certain distance. Note that you can move the slider control by placing the pointer over it and then dragging it to a new position. Alternatively, left-clicking to one side of the control results in it moving one step in that direction.

Finding the optimum setting is really a matter of trial and error. You have to be practical about things, and using a low-speed setting is not very practical if you have only a very limited amount of space for the mouse. The mouse keeps running over the edge of its allotted area, making it necessary to keep picking it up so it can be repositioned near the middle of its operating area. Lack of space is likely to be a common problem if you use a mouse with your laptop while working away from home or the office.

Mouse acceleration

Windows provides a possible solution for those requiring precise control without having a large area for the mouse. In order to activate this facility it is merely necessary to tick the "Enhance pointer precision" checkbox. This is just below the speed control. The way this system works is very simple. When the pointer is moved quickly, the mouse has its normal degree of sensitivity. This is made quite high so that relatively little mouse movement is needed in order to move the pointer around the screen.

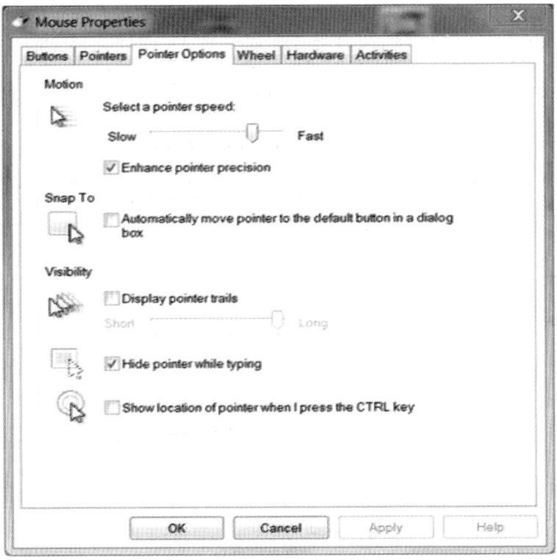

Fig.3.21 The slider controls mouse sensitivity

When the pointer is moved slowly, the sensitivity is automatically reduced so that precise positioning of the pointer is much easier. This system relies on the fact that users tend to go much more slowly and carefully when trying to position the pointer very accurately, and it can be very effective. Having two mouse sensitivities is sometimes called "mouse acceleration" incidentally. The available tabs and their windows will probably be different if you are using a mouse that has its own property window rather than the standard Microsoft type. Essentially the same controls are always present though, and it should not be too difficult to find the ones you need.

There should be a similar control program for the built-in pointing device. It can usually be accessed via an icon in the right-hand section of the taskbar at the bottom of the Windows desktop, as well as via its section in the Control Panel. However, the touchpads fitted to most portable PCs operate in a more complicated fashion than a standard three-button or wheel mouse. There are usually clever features that try to make the most of the very small usable area of the touchpad. You should therefore read the relevant section of the computer's instruction manual and learn the basics of using the touchpad before making any adjustments to its settings. When you first start using a touchpad it can give the impression that it is faulty, but the problem is usually that you are not using it correctly and do not understand some of its features.

Pressure sensitive

Some touchpads are pressure-sensitive, and there is usually a sensitivity setting for this facility. Pressure sensitivity is where the pressure on a touchpad or a graphics tablet is used to control some aspect of an application program. In paint and photo editing programs for instance, the pressure information is often used to control the width of lines produced with certain of the program's drawing and painting tools. The pressure control determines the amount of force you need to use in order to utilize a facility of this type.

There might also be a setting that controls the way in which the system operates when your finger reaches an edge of the touchpad. By necessity, the touchpad has to be quite small. It is still possible to move the pointer from one side of the screen to the other, but only if a high pointer speed is set. The problem with this approach is that it makes precise control of the pointer very difficult. Moving your finger a few millimetres produces a large amount of onscreen movement by the pointer.

Setting a much lower pointer speed gives much more precise control, but you tend to run out of space on the touchpad when moving the pointer over a large distance. Of course, you merely have to remove your finger from the pad and reposition it somewhere near the opposite edge so that you can continue moving the pointer. This is a bit slow and cumbersome though.

There is sometimes a facility that results in the pointer continuing to move even though your finger has reached the edge of the touchpad and is stationary. This enables a relatively low pointer speed to be used, and accurate control to be obtained, but large movements of the pointer are still relatively easy. How well any clever features of this type work in practice is something that you have to determine for yourself. A feature that is particularly good for one user may well be completely unusable by another user.

The exact features available tend to vary slightly from one touchpad to another, so it is a matter of reading the instruction manual to determine what special facilities, if any, are available from your computer. The instruction manual should also include details of how to control them via the Windows Control Panel. If you will be using the touchpad a great deal, it makes sense to spend some time investigating its features, trying them for yourself, and "fine tuning" any that prove to be genuinely useful. A little time spent on this type of thing can make using a laptop computer much easier and a more pleasant experience for the next few years.

Internet and networking

Getting connected

Getting any computer connected to the Internet used to be something of an ordeal, but unless you are very unlucky, these days it is reasonably straightforward. There is insufficient space available here to describe in detail the various ways of getting a PC connected to the Internet and how to deal with the problems that can arise, but the following sections cover the essentials of the main methods. There are four normal ways of getting a laptop PC connected to the Internet, which are the dial-up, wired broadband/cable, wi-fi wireless and USB dongle wireless types.

Dial-up

Until a few years ago there was no difficulty in getting a PC connected to a telephone line and using a simple dial-up connection. You simply connected the modem output of the PC to an ordinary telephone socket, and a suitable connecting lead was often supplied with the computer. If not, a standard modem lead could be obtained quite cheaply from any computer store. These days it tends to be less straightforward because a built-in modem is no longer a standard feature for desktop or portable PCs. The popularity of broadband Internet connections has presumably reduced the demand for ordinary modems to the point where it is no longer deemed worth including them as standard.

Getting connected using this method is still very simple, but you will probably need to buy a modem as an optional extra when purchasing the PC, or buy it separately. The easiest way is to buy a modem that connects to the USB port. Your Internet service provider (ISP) should provide detailed information about getting started, and they often supply a disc that makes any necessary adjustments to the setup of your computer.

This is likely to be the cheapest and easiest way of obtaining an Internet connection, but bear in mind that the speed of a dial-up connection is very slow in comparison to any form of broadband connection. A typical broadband connection is something like a hundred times faster than a good dial-up type. A dial-up connection is all right for surfing the Internet, but it is not suitable for much beyond that. Another point to keep in mind is that many dial-up services are only available from your home telephone number, and cannot be used with any telephone connection that happens to be available when you are on the move. Last, and by no means least, the telephone line cannot be used for other purposes while the dial-up connection is active. The other methods of Internet connection leave your telephone line free for normal use.

Wired broadband

Actually there are two different types of wired broadband connection, and one of these uses an ordinary telephone line plus some additional equipment connected to your telephone line at the exchange, plus some equipment to connect your computer to the telephone line. This is an ADSL (Asymmetric Digital Subscriber Line) Internet connection, and it is the most popular type. Your telephone line has to be set up for use with ADSL broadband, and a special modem is needed for an ADSL Internet link. A dial-up modem is of no use for this type of connection. An ADSL modem usually connects to the computer via a USB port or the Ethernet networking port. Some ADSL modems have provision for either method. A modem or a router is often included as part of the deal when signing up to a broadband connection. A router connects to the computer via its Ethernet port rather than a USB type, and it usually enables four or more PCs to share a broadband connection.

Slow connection

Modern ADSL connections are very fast, but bear in mind that the quoted speeds are usually the theoretical maximums and not a guaranteed minimum. In general, ADSL connections are fast if you live near to the telephone exchange, and relatively slow if you are situated a longer distance from it. ADSL broadband might not be available if you live too far from the local telephone exchange. A lower than expected ADSL connection speed is one of the most common causes for complaint in modern computing. Unfortunately, apart from moving closer to the telephone exchange there is nothing that can be done about a slow connection caused by this distance problem.

Cable

The alternative type of wired broadband connection is not strictly speaking a wired type, since the signals are carried via fibre-optic cables rather than conventional wires. This method of connection is sometimes called "cable" broadband.

Fig.4.1 A combined modem and router

It has the advantage of always working at full speed, with no dependence on the telephone exchange being a reasonably short distance away. This is due to the use of fibre-optic cables that are entirely separate from the normal telephone system. The main drawback is that this method is only available if your street has been "wired" with the fibre-optic cables.

Wireless broadband

A wireless broadband (wi-fi) connection is usually in the form of an add-on system for a wired broadband connection. Instead of a broadband modem, a combined modem and wi-fi router is used (Figure 4.1). There are sockets on this device that enable it to connect to the telephone socket and several computers via their Ethernet networking ports. There is also an aerial, or perhaps two aerials, that enable the router to connect wirelessly to computers that are equipped with a suitable wi-fi adaptor. These days an adaptor of this type is a standard feature of most laptop PCs.

The router enables several computers to share a single broadband Internet connection, with each user being able to independently access the Internet. It also enables data to be shared between any computers connected to the network. However, the network does not have to consist of the modem/router and half a dozen or more computers. It can simply comprise the modem/router and a laptop or desktop PC.

Bear in mind that having more than one PC in the network does not result in a corresponding increase in the speed of the Internet connection. The connection speed remains the same and is shared

Fig.4.2 A broadband USB dongle

between the PCs in the system. If the Internet connection is a bit slow, adding another PC effectively makes the problem worse. To misquote the old saying, "a problem shared is a problem doubled". With two PCs accessing the Internet, the connection for each computer will be twice as slow as normal, with three PCs accessing the Internet it will be three times slower than normal, and so on.

Using a wireless connection is more complicated and expensive than using a wired connection to a broadband modem, but it does have its advantages. The main one is that it is possible to use the Internet connection with the computer anywhere within a radius of about 50 metres from the modem/router. If you wish to use the Internet connection with the laptop in the garden, next-door, or an outhouse, there should be no difficulty in doing so. Just set up the laptop in the normal way and start surfing.

It is often possible to access the Internet while on the move using what are called "wireless hotspots". These offer Internet access in numerous locations around the world, with many towns and cities in the UK now having large numbers of these hotspots. A wireless hotspot is a wireless access point that connects to some form of Internet service. This will typically be a high-speed ADSL broadband connection, but it could be some other type of broadband service. It should certainly be something much faster than an ordinary dial-up connection, but bear in mind that you might have to share the service with other users, which could noticeably slow things down.

The idea is to have hotspots in restaurants, cafes, motorway service stations, hotels, trains, airports or anywhere convenient for potential users. As one would expect, these services are not usually free, and the hourly connection rates are quite high. Even so, this method can be cost-effective for those requiring Internet access on the move. The speed of the connection is also likely to be much faster than the alternatives, which are unlikely to be significantly cheaper. Some hotspots are provided free of charge, so you might get lucky from time to time and obtain free Internet access.

USB dongle

A USB broadband dongle (Figure 4.2) is a small gadget that is plugged into a USB port of your computer, and it is then possible to access the Internet via a mobile telephone network. This approach to things is not exactly new, but it has been used by relatively few people in the past due to the very high cost. Someone once calculated that the cost of downloading 20 gigabytes of music or videos would cost more than buying a typical house! The providers of mobile Internet services have had to drastically reduce their prices in order to become more competitive with alternative methods, and the cost is now more in line with these alternatives.

There are obvious attractions to a form of Internet access that can be used at home or on the move. In fact it can be used anywhere that a suitably strong signal can be obtained. Bear in mind though, that it is less than ideal if you cannot obtain a good signal when using the Internet at home, because a weak or mediocre signal will give a relatively slow connection speed. Sharing this type of interconnection can be difficult, and might not be permitted by the ISP. While downloading large amounts of data via this type of connection is far less expensive than it used to be, it could still be relatively expensive.

This type of broadband is usually capped, with a limit that is usually around one to ten gigabytes of data per month. You can go on using the connection once the monthly limit has been reached, but the additional cost for each extra megabyte is usually quite high. In fact it is usually so high that you have to keep an eye on your remaining allowance and make quite sure that it is not exceeded. Although one might hope that any unused data allowance would be carried forward to the next month, it never seems to work this way. The monthly data allowances are of the so-called "use it or lose it" variety. The cost of using this type of broadband overseas might be exhorbitant.

Wireless woes

Many of the problems with home wi-fi systems are probably due to a lack of planning. In fact most people do not seem to do any planning, and simply position everything in the system where it is most convenient from the user's point of view, rather than where it is likely to work well. Ideally there would be no problem in doing things this way, and much of the manufacturers' advertising material suggests that this approach is fine. However, in the real world it will often provide poor results from one or more parts of the system.

When using a wi-fi system it is helpful to bear in mind that this type of radio link tends to be quite pernickety. The UHF (ultra-high frequency) radio signals used by wi-fi equipment have very short wavelengths, and this can result in signals strengths varying considerably if one of the aerials is moved a small distance. Even moving an aerial a few centimetres can produce a significant change in signal strength. One reason for this is that quite small objects in the wrong place can partially block the signal. You might occasionally find that what was a very good signal suddenly becomes a noticeably weaker one. The most likely cause is that something placed closed to one of the aerials is absorbing the signal. Even someone moving slightly near one of the aerials or between two aerials can produce a dip in the signal strength.

Another problem is due to reflected signals that combine with the main signal. It is possible that the two signals will combine in a fashion that produces a boost in signal, but it is just as likely that they will have a cancelling effect, giving a reduction in the signal level. In an extreme case there can be one or more "blind" spots where there is no significant signal. Again, something being moved to just the wrong place can produce a sudden decrease in what was previously a very good signal level.

The cure in both cases is to move the aerial in an attempt to obtain a better signal level. This should not be a problem with an external wi-fi interface that connects to the PC via a cable. With a built-in interface and some form of portable computer it might be a trifle inconvenient, but it should still be possible to move the computer slightly in an attempt to obtain a better signal. Moving the aerial is clearly going to be more difficult if it is fixed to a substantial piece of equipment such as a desktop PC or a printer. In this respect built-in PC wi-fi adaptors are very restrictive, and an external USB type is more versatile.

Rather than moving the entire PC and (possibly) redesigning your office to get the wi-fi link to work well, it would probably be better to get an extension cable to permit the aerial to be positioned away from the PC. Having the aerial right next to the earthed metal case of the PC is far from ideal. Despite your best efforts it may well be in amongst some cables as well, and these will make matters worse. The truth of the matter is that the rear of a PC is just about the worst place to have a wi-fi aerial. Moving the aerial away from the cables and the PC's case will often provide much improved results. Some PCI wi-fi adaptors are now supplied with an aerial that has a built-in stand and a lead to connect it to the PC, and practical experience suggests that these are much more likely to provide good results.

The problems are much the same with a USB wi-fi adaptor that plugs straight into the back of the PC, but there is an easy solution. A USB extension cable enables the unit to be used away from the PC and will often give much better results. Note that this does not require the usual A to B lead of the type used with printers, scanners and most other USB peripherals. An A to A cable of the type used to link two PCs is not the right type either. These contain some electronics and are quite expensive. It is a simple and inexpensive A to A extension cable that is needed.

Broadband dongles can suffer from essentially the same problem. They can tend to get enmeshed with other cables, or when used with a laptop they might simply get buried in the general clutter on a table or desktop. The easy solution is the same as the one for USB wi-fi links. Connect the broadband dongle to the USB port via a short cable rather than plugging it straight into the computer. It can then be positioned where it will give good results.

Line of sight

The maximum operating ranges claimed for wi-fi equipment are often quite impressive for what is essentially a short range system. Operating ranges of over 100 metres are often claimed, and this can give the impression that there is no problem if you wish to use a wi-fi link between your house and an outbuilding at the end of a long garden, or perhaps between two houses that are about 100 metres or less apart. This type of thing is sometimes successful, but there is a high risk of the setup failing to work well, if at all.

You have to bear in mind that the claimed ranges are often for a system that is providing a line of sight link. In other words, it is only valid if there are no obstructions between the two aerials. In practice there are usually walls, trees, fences and the like between the two aerials, and these are almost certain to reduce the operating range. It should also be borne in mind that the maximum operating range is the one at which a link can be provided, and not the one at which the system will still operate at full speed. The speed of a wi-fi link reduces as the operating range is increased and the strengths of the received signals become diminished. A data link may well be possible at the quoted maximum range, but the speed obtained could be well below normal broadband speeds.

In order to obtain an effective link between two buildings it might be necessary to arrange things so that there are as few obstructions as possible between the two aerials. Having the aerials positioned outside the buildings will often improve the quality of the link, but will obviously make installing the equipment more difficult and almost certainly more costly as well. In some cases a wi-fi link might not be a practical proposition even if the two parts of the system are well within the maximum operating range quoted by the manufacturer.

Same channel?

In the United Kingdom and most of Europe there are thirteen channels available for wi-fi equipment. In theory it does not matter which channel you use for your wi-fi network, with the obvious proviso that every unit in the system must be set to use the same channel. There is no guarantee that each item in the system will use the same default channel, especially if the units are not all from the same manufacturer. It is certainly worth checking that every unit is set to the same channel number if everything seems to be set up and working correctly but one or more units in the system are failing to connect to the network.

Change channel

The small step in frequency from one channel to the next should produce no significant effect on results. The quality of the link using channel one should be the same if channel two, channel three, or any of the others are used. In practice, it is often the case that a change in channel will produce greatly improved results from a network that is underperforming. Although one channel has no technical advantage over any other channel, in a real-world situation some will usually work much better than others.

The differences in performance are almost certainly due to some channels containing more noise than others do. Another wi-fi network some distance away might not produce a resolvable signal, but it could still cause significant interference across several channels. This interference will be too weak to give problems when your wi-fi system operates at short ranges, but at long ranges the signal levels drop and the system becomes much more susceptible to interference from other systems.

Wi-fi adaptors are usually supplied with a program which lists the access points that are detected. In most cases your access point will be the only one that is listed, but inevitably some users will find that a few of their neighbours have wi-fi systems, and that these are listed as well. Try looking for access points with your own unit switched off. This will prevent it from blotting out signals from nearby systems, and increase the chances of detecting any that are present.

Clearly neither party will obtain really good results if the same channel is used for two systems. Less obviously, using adjacent channels will not improve matters very much, since wi-fi signals spread across several channels. If there are one or two other wi-fi systems in the area, use a channel that is as far removed as possible from the channel or channels that are currently in use. Some negotiation with your neighbours might be needed in order to get everyone using well separated channels.

Unfortunately, equipment other than the wi-fi variety uses the same 2.4GHz band, and it is possible that shorter than expected range is due to interference from one of these devices. Again, a change in channel might cure the problem. Moving up or down by one channel is unlikely to make much difference, because wi-fi and many other devices spread signals across several channels. A shift of about half a dozen channels is more likely to give an improvement. If necessary, try them all in order to find the one that gives optimum results. In order to change the channel used by the network it is first a matter of changing the channel used by the access point. The other units are then made to scan the band and find the access point again.

Most electronic gadgets generate electrical noise that covers a wide range of frequencies. The high operating frequency of wi-fi equipment means that it operates in a range that is well clear of most general radio noise, which is predominantly at frequencies below 100MHz (0.1GHz). However, some gadgets produce a significant signal at frequencies of more than a gigahertz. Having the access point close to a microwave oven is not a good idea, and it is probably best not to have it right next to a computer monitor.

Country setting

When installing wi-fi equipment it is normal for the user to specify the country in which the equipment will be used. This step is included when installing many pieces of software, and it is normally done simply

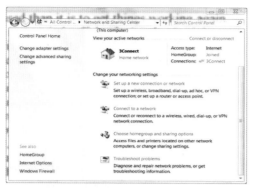

Fig.4.3 Use the Troubleshoot problems link

to ensure that menus, etc., use the appropriate language. It has this function when installing the support software for wi-fi equipment, but it also sets up the hardware so that it operates with the appropriate parameters for the country in which the equipment is being used. Although the two radio bands used for wi-fi equipment are the same for all countries, the regulations are different for each country. For instance, the channelling operates differently from one country to another.

This makes it very important to select the right country when installing wi-fi equipment. Making a mistake here could result in the equipment operating in an illegal fashion, and it might not work properly with equipment that is set up correctly. Note that when installing many programs there is no UK English option, so the US English option has to be used. The US option must not be used when installing wi-fi equipment in the UK. There should either be a UK option or one called something like "Europe Channels 1 – 13". This is the option that must be used.

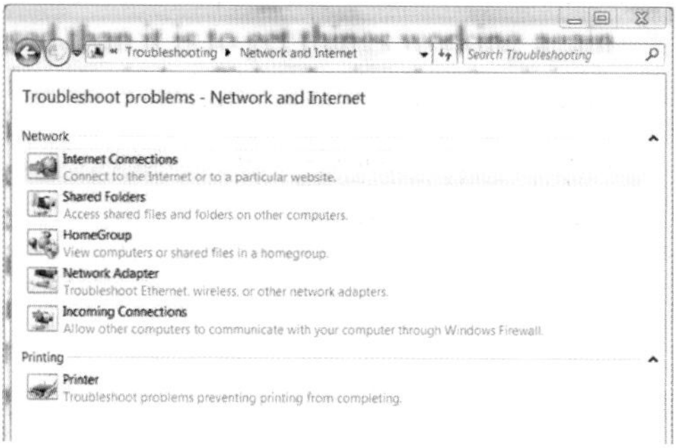

Fig.4.4 Various Internet related areas can be investigated

Repairing a connection

It does sometimes happen that a unit in the network loses its network connection and has difficulty re-establishing contact. This can be due to the system "losing the plot" rather than any physical problem. If there is a physical problem such as a detached lead, then this must be fixed before proceeding further. With the lead reconnected it is by no means certain that proper contact with the network will be established. It is easier to get the controlling software confused than it is to get things working again.

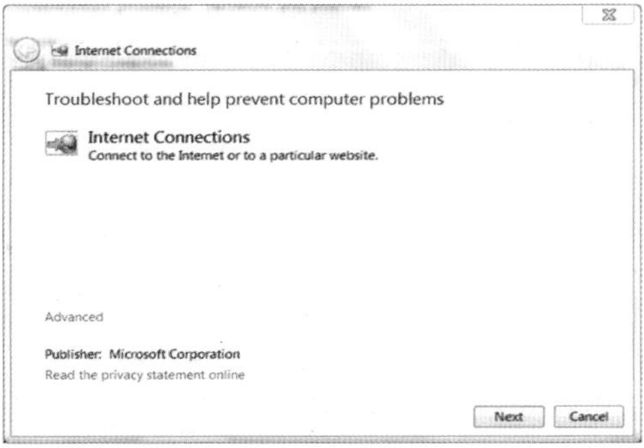

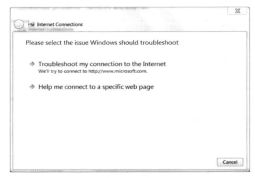

Fig.4.5 This is just an information screen

The normal way of re-establishing contact is to switch off the device that is giving problems, wait a few seconds, and then switch it on again. In an extreme case it could be necessary to switch off everything in the network, and then power it up again, one device at a time, starting with the access point. Fortunately, it is very rare for the network to get into such a state that it requires a complete restart to sort things out.

Windows 7 has a troubleshooting and repair feature that will try to re-establish contact if a network connection fails. There is no guarantee that it will work, but there is nothing to lose by trying it. Start by going to the Network and Sharing Center in an icon view of Windows Control Panel, and then Troubleshoot problems link near the bottom of the window (Figure 4.3).

There will probably be a short delay while the troubleshooter scans the system, and it will then provide a list of network related areas that can be investigated (Figure 4.4). The obvious one to try first is the Internet Connections link, and selecting this will produce the

Fig.4.6 Use the upper icon or link

information screen of Figure 4.5. Operating the Next button will move things on to the window of Figure 4.6, and here it is the upper option that should be selected. The troubleshooter will then investigate the problem and report that the connection has been repaired, suggest actions that might cure the problem, or give the reason why it failed to repair the problem, as appropriate.

Download managers

When downloading large files from the Internet there can be problems with broken downloads. This is where everything starts well and the file downloads correctly for some time, but things then grind to a halt. This is usually caused by the sending and receiving ends of the system briefly losing contact and then being unable to re-establish contact. The download facility of your browser might have the ability to regain contact with the server and start downloading again from where it left off, but in some cases it is a matter of starting again from scratch.

With any sort of wireless link you have to accept the occasional broken download as a fact of wireless life. If it keeps occurring it is likely that you are stretching the range of the system slightly, and reliable downloading might be impossible unless you can improve the signal strength. Problems when downloading also have to be accepted as a fact of computing life when using a dial-up connection. Dial-up connections push an ordinary telephone line right to its limits, and reliability tends to suffer as a result of this. With some form of wired or cable broadband there should be no more than the occasional problem when downloading. If there are frequent problems it is probably best to report the problem to your Internet service provider (ISP), as there could well be a problem in the connection from your premises to the provider's equipment.

There are programs that are designed to manage and in some cases speed up downloads. Programs of this type are generally called download managers. One advantage of these programs is that they will usually be able to resume a broken download, carrying on from the point at which the download stopped. The built-in download facility of a browser might lack this facility, making it necessary to start again from the beginning if the connection to the server is lost. Note though, that any facility to resume a broken download can only work if it is supported by the equipment at both ends of the link. Therefore, the fact that you are using a download manager does not mean that it will always be possible to resume broken downloads. Fortunately, these days the vast majority of servers support this feature.

Index

A

acceleration 104
Action Center 49
ADSL 108
aerial 110
anti-malware 53
Appearance and Personalization 84
automatic restart 48
Automatic Updates 4

B

backup 12, 31
battery 83, 96
boot disc 37
boot drive 13
broadband 22, 108
broken downloads 118

C

cable 109
cache 22
calibration 77
channel 114
click speed 103
CMOS 28
Colors menu 86
Command Prompt 44, 47
Computer 14
configuration files 7
Control Panel 36, 84, 86, 89, 102
Control-Alt-Escape 24
country setting 115

D

Debugging Mode 48
defragmenters 8
deleting 90
Devices and Printers 69
dial-up 107
disc bloat 11
disc drives 9

D (continued)

Disk Cleanup 18
dongle 111
download managers 118
downloads 6
Driver Signature 49
driver software 25, 79
DVD drive 64
DVI 63

E

Ease of Access Center 93
Email scanner 57
Enable Boot Logging 48
End Process 27
Ethernet 109

F

freeing jams 67

G

Good Configuration 48
gsm 66

H

hackers 53
hardware problem 41
hotspots 110
hub 62

I

installation disc 38
installation program 91
Internet 22, 107
Internet Explorer 21

K

keyboard 59, 95

L

laptops 81
line of sight 80, 113
logical disc 9
low-resolution 48

M

Magnifier	94
malware	52
memory	43
memory effect	98
modem	109
mouse	59, 101

N

Narrator	95
notebooks	81

O

operating system	3

P

paper jams	64
paper path	68
partition	10
PDF	74
power-on self-test	27
pressure sensitive	106
print heads	76
print quality	74
printer driver	71

R

rebooting	6
Recovery Tools	39, 40
Recycle Bin	15, 23
Registry	58
repair disc	35
Repair Your Computer	46
reset button	2
Restore	40
restore points	30
router	109
reconnecting	80

S

Safe Mode	34, 46
scan	56
scan rate	87
screen resolution	83

self test	72
Setup program	28
Shut down	2
shutdown problems	24
slow printing	73
Start button	1
Start menu	2, 14
Start Windows Normally	45
Start-up problems	27
Startup Repair	44
streaky printing	75
System Properties	35
system repair disc	35
System Restore	29, 32

T

Task Manager	24, 25
temporary files	23
temporary Internet files	19
test pages	68
text	88
toner cartridge	75
troubleshooter	51

U

uninstaller	8, 92
updates	4
UPS	99
USB drive	12
USB power	61
USB types	60
Using F8	45

V

VGA	63
video	63
virus	53

W

wi-fi	109
Windows Explorer	22
Windows Registry	58
wireless peripheral	78